Sky 3

Activity Book

Ingrid Freebairn
Hilary Rees-Parnall
Jonathan Bygrave
Brian Abbs

What's happening?

Present simple

1 Look at the pictures of Sam. Then write full questions and the answers.

1 What time / Sam / get up?
What time does Sam get up?
He gets up at eight o'clock.

2 Have / an egg for breakfast?
Does Sam have an egg for breakfast?
NO Sam does not.

3 Ride / his bike to school?
Does Sam ride his bike to school?
NO sam walks to school.

4 What time / finish school?
What time does Sam finish school?
He finishes at 3:30

5 What / usually do after school?
What does he usually do after school?
He plays football.

6 What time / go to bed?
What time does he go to bed?
Sam goes to bed at 9:30

Present continuous

2 Complete the questions and answers.

1 A: Hi Kenny! What ¹*are you doing* (you / do)?
B: I ² *am watching* (watch) a film.

2 A: Look out!
B: Why? What ³ .... (I / do)?
A: You ⁴ .... (stand) on my magazine!

3 A: Look! There's Nicole Kidman.
B: What ⁵ .... (she / do)?
A: She ⁶ .... (come) out of the theatre. She ⁷ .... (sign) autographs.

4 A: Hi, Lotty. It's me, Rosie. What are you and Charlie doing? ⁸ .... (you / have) a cola?
B: No, ⁹ .... (we / not / have) a cola, ¹⁰ .... (we / eat) a pizza!

Present simple / Present continuous

3 Circle the correct words.

Johhny Mac

Johnny Mac is a pop star. He ¹*plays* / *is playing* the lead guitar in the band Proxy. He ²*comes* / *is coming* from Glasgow in Scotland. At the moment Johnny and the other members of the band ³*live* / *are living* in London and ⁴*make* / *are making* a video. Johnny is only fifteen and still ⁵*goes to* / *is going to* school. In his free time, he ⁶*writes* / *is writing* poems and songs. Right now he ⁷*writes* / *is writing* a new song for Proxy's next album.

Personal information

4a Complete the conversation.

do you come   Cool!   too
~~Excuse me~~   does   Where   works
live   this   What's

Sam: ¹ *Excuse me*, is this free?
Ricky: Sure.
Sam: Where ² .... from?
Ricky: We come from New York in the USA.
Sam: ³ .... do you live in New York?
Ricky: We ⁴ .... near Central Park.
Sam: ⁵ ....

Gina: Dad's got a job here in England.
Sam: Where ⁶ .... he work?
Ricky: He ⁷ .... in the centre of London.
Sam: ⁸ .... your name?
Ricky: I'm Ricky. And ⁹ .... is my sister, Gina.
Sam: Hi, Gina. I've got a sister, ¹⁰ .... Her name's Lucy.

4b Write the questions.

Ricky: ¹ *What's your name* ?
Sam: My name's Sam.
Ricky: ² ....
Sam: My sister? Her name's Lucy.
Ricky: ³ .... ?
Sam: We live in West london.
Ricky: ⁴ .... ?
Sam: We both go to Putney High School.
Ricky: ⁵ .... ?
Sam: Skateboarding? Yes, I do. I love it.
Ricky: ⁶ .... to do some skateboarding this afternoon?
Sam: Yes. Great!

Places in town

5 Find the hidden places.

1 g a r c i n e m a d e n
2 d o s c a f e m a r t
3 v e r i c a r p a r k o r t
4 m a c r e s t a u r a n t i d
5 w i n b o o k s h o p i a l
6 p r i n s t a t i o n y c
7 r e t a p o s t o f f i c e t o n

Which one?

Money

1a Look at the pictures. Write the prices.

1 The big bag is ten pounds.
2 The sunglasses with the black frames are eighteen pounds fifty pence.
3 ....
4 ....
5 ....
6 ....

one / ones

1b Look at the pictures again. Write conversations about the objects with a price.

1 A: I like that bag.
  B: Which one?
  A: The big one.
2 A: I like those sunglasses.
  B: Which ones?
  A: The ones with the black frames.
3 A: I like ....
  B: ....
  A: ....
4 A: I like ....
  B: ....
  A: ....
5 A: I like ....
  B: ....
  A: ....
6 A: I like ....
  B: ....
  A: ....

Shopping

2 Complete the conversation.

Lucy: Excuse me, ¹ *how much* are the sunglasses?
Man: Which ² .... ?
Lucy: The ³ .... black frames.
Man: They're £14.95.
Lucy: OK. ⁴ .... them, please.
Man: Sure. ⁵ .... are.
Lucy: ⁶ ....

Future plans and intentions

3 Complete the conversations with the *going to* form of the verb.

1 A: I ¹ *'m going to go* (go) shopping this afternoon.
   B: What ² .... (you / buy)?
   A: I ³ .... (buy) some new trainers.
   B: ⁴ .... (your mum / buy) them for you?
   A: Yes, she ⁵ .... (buy) me some trainers and a T-shirt.

2 A: What ⁶ .... (you two / have)?
   B: We ⁷ .... (have) a cola but we ⁸ .... (not / have) anything to eat.

3 A: ⁹ .... (you / come) to the market with me?
   B: Yes, I am. Hang on! I want to put on my new anorak. It ¹⁰ .... (rain).

Future arrangements

4 Choose and write complete answers.

1 A: What time is your grandmother arriving?
   B: [d] *She's arriving at ten o'clock.*
2 A: What time are you having lunch on Sunday?
   B: ☐ ....
3 A: Where are you meeting them?
   B: ☐ ....
4 A: When is your brother leaving school?
   B: ☐ ....
5 A: When are AC Milan playing FC Porto?
   B: ☐ ....
6 A: Who are your parents staying with when they go to Italy?
   B: ☐ ....

a They ...... them on Saturday.
b We ...... it at two o'clock.
c They ...... with Dad's cousin.
d She ...... at ten o'clock.
e He ...... in January.
f I ...... them outside the bank.

5 Circle the right verb phrase.

1 Have a look in my diary. What time is Sarah *arriving* / *going to arrive*?
2 A: Where's Mark?
   B: I don't know. I *'m phoning* / *'m going to phone* him.
3 You need an umbrella. It *rains* / *'s going to rain* later.
4 Maths is so hard! I *'m not passing* / *'m not going to pass* the exam.
5 I can't find my keys. What *are we doing* / *are we going to do*?
6 Remember – your grandmother *comes* / *is coming* this afternoon.
7 Don't go and see that film. You *aren't enjoying* / *aren't going to enjoy* it.

5

3 We made friends.

The past simple: positive

1 Complete the letter. Choose a verb and write the past simple form.

go	make	~~arrive~~
have	see	buy	give
meet	want	take

Dear Aunt Judy,

Thanks very much for the Harry Potter book. It ¹ _arrived_ two days ago, just in time for my birthday. When Sam ² .... it, he ³ .... to read it immediately!

I ⁴ .... a nice birthday. Mum and Dad ⁵ .... me some money so I ⁶ .... into town yesterday and ⁷ .... a digital camera. I ⁸ .... a photo of Sam in his pyjamas. Here it is!

A few weeks ago I ⁹ .... an American girl called Beth and ¹⁰ .... friends with her. She's really nice. I must stop now. Thank you again!

Love from
Lucy

The past simple: questions and negative

2a Write the conversations. Use the cues.

1 you / see Daniel? // Ron
 A: _Did you see Daniel?_
 B: _No, I didn't see Daniel. I saw Ron._

2 he / write a letter? // postcard
 A: ....
 B: ....

3 you / find her address? // phone number
 A: ....
 B: ....

4 they / come this morning? // at lunchtime
 A: ....
 B: ....

5 she / forget her books? // pencil case
 A: ....
 B: ....

6 he / say hello? // goodbye
 A: ....
 B: ....

6

2b Complete the conversation.

Sam: I ¹ *didn't have* (not / have) a very good day at school yesterday.

Ricky: Why? What happened? ² .... (you / forget) to take your mobile phone?

Sam: No. I ³ .... (forget) my Maths homework! I ⁴ .... (go back) home and I ⁵ .... (find) it under my bed. Our dog Rex ⁶ .... (have) it in his mouth!

Ricky: What ⁷ .... (your teacher / say)?

Sam: She ⁸ .... (not / say) very much. I just ⁹ .... (say) sorry and ¹⁰ .... (go) to my desk.

ago

3 Answer the questions with *ago*. First look at the time and date now.

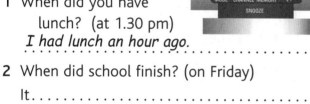

1 When did you have lunch? (at 1.30 pm)
  I had lunch an hour ago.

2 When did school finish? (on Friday)
  It....................................

3 When did your grandmother arrive? (on Sunday July 3rd)
  She..................................

4 When did you buy those jeans? (in May)
  I....................................

5 When did your brother meet Julie? (in 2001)
  He....................................

6 When did the match start? (at 2.10 pm)
  It....................................

Free time activities

4a Write *the* where necessary.

1 watch ...... television
2 go to *the* cinema
3 listen to ...... music
4 go ...... swimming
5 play ...... guitar
6 play ...... football
7 go to ...... theatre
8 listen to ...... radio

4b Now match the phrases in 4a with the pictures A–H below.

1	C	2		3		4	
5		6		7		8	

Skills practice

Reading

1 Read about the places. Match the texts with the pictures.

Ben [ ] Ryan [ ] Emma [ ]

New words
lean
look as if

Picture A

Picture B

Picture C

I saw the Eiffel Tower in Paris when I visited France last year on a school trip. I learnt a lot about it. My teacher said it took two years to build. It opened in 1889. She also said that about six million people visit it every year. It was very busy when we were there. It's 324 metres high. There are 1665 steps to the top but we went up by lift.
(Ben, 13)

I live in Sydney in Australia and I see Sydney Harbour Bridge every day when I go to school. It joins north and south Sydney. My grandfather remembers when it opened in 1932. He says it took six years to build. It is 1149 metres long and 49 metres wide. You can walk or cycle across it and cars and trains use it, too. You can even climb up it!
(Ryan, 12)

When I was on holiday in Italy we visited Pisa and saw the Leaning Tower. It's very funny! It took about two hundred years to build. It's 55 metres high. At first it was straight and then it began to lean to one side. Now it looks as if it's going to fall over. Perhaps one day it will. Lots of people go to see it and take photos like mine!
(Emma, 14)

2a Complete the sentences with the correct place name.

1 *Sydney Harbour Bridge* opened in 1932.
2 .... took two years to build.
3 .... took six years to build.
4 .... took about two hundred years to build.
5 .... has 1665 steps.
6 .... is 55 metres high.
7 .... is 324 metres high.
8 .... is 49 metres wide.

2b Answer the questions.

1 Where did Ben go on a school trip?
   He went to France.
2 How many people visit the Eiffel Tower every year?
   ....
3 Where does Ryan live?
   ....
4 When did the bridge open?
   ....
5 Where did Emma go on holiday?
   ....
6 What did she see?
   ....

Listening

3 🎧 Listen and match each person with the place they live and what they like doing.

Daisy		a playing with the dog
	Yorkshire	b going to concerts
Sarah	Edinburgh	c looking at the sea
	Devon	d meeting friends
Fraser		e riding a bike
		f walking on the beach

Daisy ....
Sarah ....
Fraser ....

Writing tip
Do you remember how to end a letter or postcard? Check in your *Students' Book*.

4 Will and Alice are on holiday in different places. Look at the pictures, then write a letter from each of them in your notebook.

Dear Mum and Dad,
I'm having a horrible / brilliant time here.

(weather) (food) (friends) (home)

Cartoon Time:
Clark and Lois – school reporters

5 Complete the conversation with the words in the box.

| silly   Excuse   Hang   Quick   happening |
| change   ~~Look~~   Hurry |

Lois: We need a good story for the school newspaper.
Clark: ¹ *Look.* There's the hot dog vendor. What's ² .... ?
Lois: Someone is stealing a hot dog.

Clark: ³ .... ! Stop him. Great!
Lois: Take a picture. ⁴ .... up!
Clark: Why did you steal the hot dog?

Vendor: ⁵ .... me, sir. Here's your ⁶ ....
Man: Thanks.
Lois: ⁷ .... on! Isn't he stealing a hot dog?
Vendor: Don't be ⁸ .... He's my best customer.

5 Check   Lessons 1–4

1 Complete the conversation.

A: Where ¹ *do you come from* (you / come from) ?

B: We ² .... (come from) New York.

A: What ³ .... (happen)?

B: We ⁴ .... (wait) to see Will Smith!

A: ⁵ .... (he / be) American?

B: Yes, but he ⁶ .... (stay) in London at the moment.

A: How ⁷ .... (he / usually spend) his free time?

B: He ⁸ .... (ride) around in his Jeep.

Score ___ /7

2 Write answers with *one* or *ones*.

1 Which bag do you like? (big)
 I like the big one.

2 Which sunglasses do you like? (black frames)
 .... with the ....

3 Which mobile phone do you like? (pink)
 ....

4 Which apples do you like? (green)
 ....

5 Which trainers do you like? (purple and white)
 ....

6 Which bag do you like? (blue stars)
 .... with the .... on it.

7 Which socks do you like? (moon and stars)
 .... with the .... on them.

8 Which T-shirt do you like? (yellow cat)
 .... with the .... on it.

Score ___ /7

3 Write the prices in words.

1 *One pound seventy-two.*

2 ....

3 ....

4 ....

5 ....

6 ....

Score ___ /5

10

4 What are they going to do tomorrow? Match each picture with an activity and write sentences with *going to*.

lie on the beach   ~~see a film~~   play football
go shopping   watch television
go skateboarding

1 Anna *is going to see a film.*
2 Millie ....
3 Nick ....
4 Jack and Kate ....
5 Mike ....
6 I ....

Score ___ /5

5 Read the text about Orlando Bloom and put the verbs into the simple past.

Orlando Bloom
1 ... *grew* ... (grow) up in the UK in Canterbury.
He 2 .... (leave) school at sixteen and 3 .... (go) to London. He 4 .... (study) at the Guildhall School of Music and Drama for three years. In 1998 he 5 .... (fall) out of a window and 6 .... (break) his back. Fortunately he 7 .... (get) better quickly. After studying at the Guildhall he 8 .... (begin) work on the film 'Lord of the Rings'. He 9 .... (spend) eighteen months filming in New Zealand. While he 10 .... (be) there, he 11 .... (learn) to surf.

Score ___ /10

6 Complete Sally's letter to her parents. Write in the places where she went.

Dear Mum and Dad,
I arrived here in Brighton on Monday. I caught the train from London and Aunt Susan met me at the 1 s*tation* . Yesterday I changed some money at the 2 b............... . In the morning we all went shopping. Aunt Susan went to the 3 s............... to buy food, but Milly and I didn't buy anything. In the afternoon we went to the 4 c............... to see the new Brad Pitt film. It was really good. In the evening we ate in a 5 r............... and then we went to a 6 d............... . We danced all night. It was fun! I must stop now and take this to the 7 p............... o............... .
With love,
Sally

Score ___ /6

CHECK YOUR SCORE!

TOTAL ___ /40

☐ Brilliant! (30–40)
☐ Good! (20–29)
☐ OK (10–19)

He could draw well.

Verbs of action

1 Solve the clues to complete the word puzzle.

Across
1 Can I use your c................ please? (8)
3 I can't snowboard or _skateboard_ . (10)
4 How do you .... your name? (5)
6 You must .... this book. It's very good. (4)
7 I haven't got a bike. Let's .... (4)
8 Can she .... the time? (4)

Down
2 Joshua can .... pictures very well. (4)
3 I learnt to .... in the sea. (4)
5 I'm going to .... my room blue. (5)
6 Can you .... a horse? (4)
7 Please .... your name here. (5)
8 Ssh! Don't .... (4)
9 Can you .... the piano? (4)

could / couldn't (ability)

2a Make sentences about William.

1 _When William was six months old, he could smile but he couldn't talk._
2 When he was one,
....
3 ....
....
4 ....
....
5 ....
....
6 ....
....
7 ....

Aged 6 mths	Aged 1	Aged 4	Aged 5	Aged 6	Aged 8	Aged 10
smile ✓ talk ✗	walk ✓ run ✗	count to 50 ✓ tell the time ✗	do up his shoes ✓ do up his buttons ✗	read and write ✓ draw ✗	ride a bike ✓ swim ✗	use a computer ✓ play the piano ✗

2b Complete the text with *could* or *couldn't*.

The wild girl

One day in 1731 some people in a village in France found a wild girl in a tree. She was about ten years old. She was frightened and she ¹ ..*couldn't*.. speak. She ² .... only shout and cry. She lived in the woods and she ³ .... run and swim well. The people called her Memmie le Blanc. She liked bread and vegetables. She ⁴ .... eat raw meat, but she ⁵ .... eat cooked meat. She learnt to speak a little French but she ⁶ .... speak more than twenty words. Who was she? Nobody knows for certain.

when and *after*

3 Complete the conversation with *could* or *couldn't*.

Gina: Excuse me, where is Green Park tube station?
Man: xxxxxx.
Ricky: What did he say?
Gina: I don't know. I ¹ ..*couldn't*.. understand him. ² .... you?
Ricky: No, I ² ....
Gina: Let's ask this woman. Excuse me, where is Green Park tube station?
Woman: xxxxxxdilly.
Gina: Er ... Thank you.
Ricky: She said it so fast! I ⁴ .... hear the name of the street. ⁵ .... you hear it?
Gina: Yes, I ⁶ .... She said 'Piccadilly'. That's the name of a street near here.

4 Join the sentences with *when* and *after*.

When

1 He was six. He could swim.
   When he was six, he could swim.

2 I was only seven. I learnt to speak Spanish.
   ....

3 He was sixty. He bought a motorbike.
   ....

4 She started school. She couldn't read or write.
   ....

After

5 He left school. His parents moved to Italy.
   ....

6 The programme finished. They went to bed.
   ....

7 She saw the film. She couldn't sleep.
   ....

7 We were driving ...

Prepositions of motion

1 Complete the instructions with the correct preposition.

| into | round | out of | across | past |
| through | ~~along~~ | under | over | |

First you ride ¹ *along* the banks of the River Dee, ² .... Farmer's Cottage. Then turn right and ride ³ .... Beechy Woods. After the woods, you come to a big field. Go ⁴ .... the field to the other side and ⁵ .... a car park. You come ⁶ .... the car park on the south side. After that, you go ⁷ .... the Roman Viaduct and ⁸ .... Freshwater Lake. After the lake you go ⁹ .... a bridge to the Finish Line. Good luck!

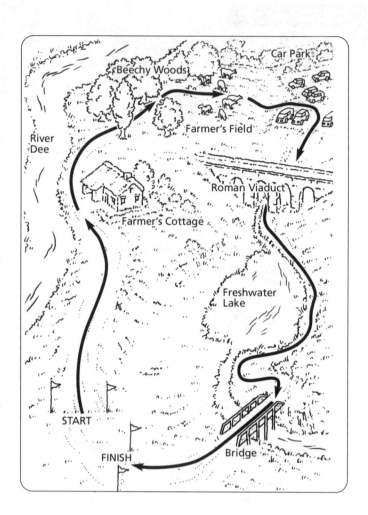

Past simple and past continuous

2a Complete the conversation. Write the past simple or past continuous forms of the verbs.

A: Guess what ¹ *happened* (happen) last night.

B: What?

A: We ² .... (have) a power cut!

B: Really? What ³ .... (you / do) at the time?

A: I ⁴ .... (have) a shower, my sister ⁵ .... (play) on her computer, and my mum and dad ⁶ .... (watch) TV.

B: I remember last year at school all the lights ⁷ .... (go out) while we ⁸ .... (do) a Maths test. It was great!

2b Choose the correct verb form.

Sharks Ahoy!

Last summer we [1] *spent* / *were spending* our summer holidays in Cornwall. One morning, while our parents [2] *shopped* / *were shopping*, my sister Lucy and I [3] *went* / *were going* to the beach. We [4] *played* / *were playing* volleyball when suddenly I [5] *saw* / *was seeing* a shark's fin in the water. A shark [6] *swam* / *was swimming* in the sea near the beach! We immediately [7] *ran* / *were running* across the beach to the coastguard's hut. 'Don't worry,' he [8] *said* / *was saying*, 'they aren't dangerous man-eating sharks!' But Lucy was terrified. She [9] *didn't want* / *wasn't wanting* to swim in the sea again!

when and while

3a Write *when* or *while* in the sentences.

1. The helicopter flew past ....*while*.... we were swimming in the river.
2. The boys were walking through some woods .... they saw a snake.
3. Maria was having breakfast .... her mobile phone started to ring.
4. .... I was doing my homework, I listened to my new CD.
5. My little brother's tooth came out .... he was eating a biscuit.
6. Dad was cleaning his car .... he found a £20 note under the seat.

3b Join the sentences with *when* and *while*.

1. I / shop in the market // somebody / steal my wallet

   While I was shopping in the market, somebody stole my wallet.

   I was shopping in the market when somebody stole my wallet.

2. we / have dinner // the police / knock at the door

   ....
   ....

3. Colleen / buy a magazine // see her teacher

   ....
   ....

4. Hugo / clear the table // break a glass

   ....
   ....

He used to play the drums.

Musical instruments

1 Wordsearch – find the names of ten musical instruments in this word puzzle.

<u>acoustic guitar</u>

```
S K E Y B O A R D S
A A D R O M C I R A
C T R O M B O N E X
O R U M S A F A C O
U U M U S I L V O P
S M S F A R U I R H
T P I A N O T O D O
I E L R W C E L E N
C T O P U D N I R E
G U I T A R K N E T
```

used to

2a Look at the pictures and choose a verb. Then write sentences with *used to* and *didn't use to*. This is DDKing today. What was he like before he was a famous pop star?

| live   eat   spend |
| play   ~~have~~   have |

1 dark hair / blond hair
<u>He used to have dark hair. He didn't use</u>
<u>to have blond hair.</u>

2 wavy hair / straight hair
....
....

3 in the country / in the centre of London
....
....

4 fish and chips every day / foreign food
....
....

5 the piano / the guitar
....
....

6 his holidays in Britain / his holidays abroad
....
....

2b Write *used to* or *didn't use to* in the gaps.

My grandfather

My grandfather was born in 1925. He ¹ *used to* live in Wales. He ² .... go to school in a village five kilometres away. There ³ .... be any buses so he ⁴ .... walk to school. He ⁵ .... wear short trousers to school, even in winter! He married my grandmother in 1953. When they were first married, they were quite poor and they ⁶ .... have a car. In the evening they ⁷ .... read books and play the piano. They ⁸ .... watch television because only very rich people had them.

3 Complete the conversation. Choose a word from the box.

| used to   Did   did   ~~used~~   didn't use to |
| didn't   Did she use |

A: That's a photo of my mum when she was nineteen. She ¹ *used* to have blonde hair. And that's her guitar.

B: Wow! ² .... to play the guitar?

A: Yes, she ³ .... It was an acoustic guitar, not an electric guitar. She ⁴ .... sing too. Dad says she was brilliant.

B: ⁵ .... she use to play in a band?

A: No, she ⁶ .... She ⁷ .... like performing in public.

4 Complete the conversation. Choose a word or phrase from the box.

| really not bad.   hopeless   ~~Come on!~~ |
| Not really.   Must you?   didn't use to |
| didn't use to   Here goes! |
| Don't be so mean!   not any more. |
| used to   trumpet |

Ricky: ¹ *Come on!* Play a tune on the piano.

Sam: OK. ² ....

Lucy: Oh Sam. ³ .... I'm trying to do my homework. Anyway, you're ⁴ .... at the piano.

Sam: ⁵ .... Do you play any instruments, Ricky?

Ricky: ⁶ .... I used to have guitar lessons but ⁷ ....

Lucy: Why not?

Ricky: Well, I ⁸ .... practise so I was never very good. But my brother's different. He ⁹ .... win music prizes and now he plays the ¹⁰ .... in a jazz band.

Sam: Is he good?

Ricky: Yes, he's ¹¹ ....

Sam: Do you like jazz?

Ricky: Yes, I do. I ¹² .... like it but I do now.

Skills practice

New words

amphibian   develop
evolution   fierce
heading   meteor
reptile   skin   spike

Reading

1 Read the article.

DINOSAURS

Dinosaurs lived on earth a long time ago. The first dinosaurs appeared 225 million years ago, before there were any people. Today there are no dinosaurs. They disappeared 65 million years ago. People appeared on earth about three million years ago, a long time after the dinosaurs died out.

All living things change. This process is called evolution. No animals lived on land 350 million years ago. Then some fish left the water. They developed legs and became amphibians, animals which can live in water or on land. They laid eggs. About 40 million years later, they became reptiles, like lizards or crocodiles. They grew thick skin to protect them from the sun. Eventually, about 80 million years later, some of them developed stronger and straighter legs and became the first dinosaurs.

Stegosaurus

Tyrannosaurus Rex

We don't know why the dinosaurs disappeared. Some people say the weather changed. Others say the dinosaurs grew too big. Many scientists think a meteor hit the earth and the world became cold and dark. All the dinosaurs died and no new ones evolved. It was the end of the dinosaur age.

2a True (✓) or False (✗)?

1 People lived on earth before dinosaurs. ✗
2 Dinosaurs lived on earth for about 160 million years. ☐
3 Dinosaurs disappeared 230 million years ago. ☐
4 All living things change. ☐
5 Dinosaurs evolved from reptiles. ☐
6 We know why the dinosaurs disappeared. ☐

2b Number these sentences in the correct order.

a People appeared on earth. ☐
b Some fish left the water. ☐
c Dinosaurs disappeared. ☐
d The first dinosaurs appeared. ☐
e Reptiles evolved. ☐
f No animals lived on land. 1

3 Choose the best heading for the three paragraphs in Exercise 1. (You do not need to use all the headings.)

Who discovered dinosaurs? ☐
How did dinosaurs evolve? ☐
Where did dinosaurs live? ☐
When did dinosaurs appear? ☐ 1
Why did dinosaurs disappear? ☐
What did dinosaurs eat? ☐

Writing

4 Look at the information about the Stegosaurus and complete the text.

Stegosaurus: 4 legs/9 metres long/7 metres tall/spikes on back/ate plants/lived in North America and Africa

The Stegosaurus was a big dinosaur. It had
¹ *four* legs. It was ² .... metres long and ³ .... metres tall. It had ⁴ .... on its back. It ate ⁵ .... It lived in ⁶ ....

5 Now write two paragraphs about the Brachiosaurus and the Tyrannosaurus Rex in your notebook.

Brachiosaurus: biggest dinosaur/4 legs/30 metres long/12 metres tall/ate plants/lived in North America and Africa

Tyrannosaurus Rex: fiercest dinosaur/4 legs/15 metres long/ 5 metres tall/sharp teeth/ate meat/lived in North America and Canada

The Brachiosaurus was the biggest dinosaur.
....

The Tyrannosaurus Rex was the fiercest dinosaur.
....

Cartoon Time:
Clark and Lois – school reporters

6 Complete the conversation with the words in the box.

| Come hopeless ~~really~~ goes Must more |

Clark: How are we going to get £20? It's impossible.
Lois: Not ¹ *really* . Can you play a musical instrument?
Clark: Not any ² .... I used to play the violin.

Clark: This is a bad idea. I was ³ .... at the violin.
Lois: ⁴ .... on! Think about the school newspaper.
Clark: OK. Here ⁵ ....

Woman: ⁶ .... you?
Lois: We need money for our school newspaper.
Woman: Here's 50p. Please go away.

10 Check Lessons 6–9

1 Match the verbs of action.

1 write — a the time
2 use   b a picture
3 ride   c a computer
4 spell   d the guitar
5 tell   e a word
6 play   f a bike
7 draw   g an essay

1 g 2 ___
3 ___ 4 ___
5 ___ 6 ___
7 ___

Score ___ /6

2 Choose the correct phrase from the box and complete the sentences with could / couldn't.

she / play the guitar really well.
I / understand.   we / watch it.
I / go on holiday.   ~~he / walk again.~~
they / speak a word!

3 Complete the sentences with a preposition from the box.

~~across~~   along   around
into   over   under

1 You can cycle *across* Sydney Harbour Bridge.
2 My dog hates storms – he hides .... my bed!
3 The teacher came .... the classroom.
4 Explorers travel .... the world.
5 I met my friends as I was walking .... the road.
6 The helicopter flew .... our heads.

Score ___ /5

1 Six months after the accident *he could walk again.*

2 They studied French for six years but ....

3 She never had any lessons but ....

4 I lost my passport so ....

5 He spoke very slowly so ....

6 The television was broken so ....

Score ___ /5

20

4 Write sentences using *when*.

1 I / wash / my hair // phone / ring
   I was washing my hair when the phone rang.

2 They / watch / television // we / arrive
   ....

3 Ben / swim / in the sea // see / a shark
   ....

4 We / have / picnic // it / start / to rain
   ....

5 My sister / play / tennis // fell over
   ....

6 We / have / a party // our parents / come home
   ....

Score ___ /5

5 Now write the sentences again in your notebook, using *while*.

1 *The phone rang while I was washing my hair.*

Score ___ /5

6 Find nine instruments.

1 T r u m p e t
2 _ l _ _ _ _
3 _ r _ _ _
4 _ _ _ _ _ _ _ n
5 _ _ _ _ _ _ _ r
6 G _ _ _ _ _ _
7 _ i _ _ _ _
8 V _ _ _ _ _ _
9 _ _ x _ _ _ _ _ _

Score ___ /8

7 Jemma is talking to her grandmother. Complete their conversation with the correct form of *used to*.

Jemma: ¹ *Did you use to have* (you / have) lots of toys, Gran?

Gran: No, ² *we used to invent* (we / invent) our own games.

Jemma: ³ .... (people / travel) to other countries?

Gran: Oh no, ⁴ .... (people / not travel) very often.

Jemma: ⁵ .... (your parents / have) a car?

Gran: No, ⁶ .... (they / not have) a car. ⁷ .... (We / walk) everywhere.

Jemma: Is life easier now?

Gran: Yes, it is. But ⁸ .... (we / have) a lot of fun!

Score ___ /6

CHECK YOUR SCORE!

TOTAL ___ /40

☐ Brilliant! (30–40)
☐ Good! (20–29)
☐ OK (10–19)

21

11 They're too casual.

Clothes, patterns and styles

1a Complete the labels for the dogs' coats.

1 a <u>s t r i p e d</u> coat
2 a <u>s p _ t _ _ d</u> coat
3 a <u>p l _ _ n</u> coat
4 a <u>f l _ w _ _ _ y</u> coat
5 a <u>c h _ _ k _ d</u> coat
6 a <u>p _ t t _ _ n _ d</u> coat.

1b Label the clothes in the picture.

1 tracksuit
2 ....
3 ....
4 ....
5 ....
6 ....
7 ....
8 ....
9 ....

Adjective + enough

2 Write sentences with an adjective and *enough*.

1 (she / tall)
She isn't tall enough.

2 (he / old)
....

3 (they / smart)
....

4 (it / long)
....

too + adjective

3 Complete the conversations with *too* and the adjective under the picture.

1 A: *What do you think of this coat?* .... (coat)
 B: *It's too smart.*
2 A: *What do you think of these sandals?* .... (sandals)
 B: *They're too casual.*
3 A: .... (mini-skirt)
 B: ....
4 A: .... (tracksuit)
 B: ....
5 A: .... (sweater)
 B: ....
6 A: .... (belt)
 B: ....

1 s m a r t   2 c a s u a l

3 _ h _ _ _   4 _ _ _ _ y

5 _ _ _ h _   6 _ _ _ _ e

too and enough

4 Write sentences using *too* or *enough*.

1 He can't learn to drive. He's only sixteen. (He / old)
 He isn't old enough.

2 These trousers are no good. You need a bigger size. (They / tight)
 ....

3 I don't want to swim in the sea. (It / warm).
 ....

4 I'm not going to buy that tracksuit. It costs £60. (It / expensive)
 ....

5 This car isn't fast enough. (It / slow)
 ....

6 You can't wear those sandals to the wedding. (They / smart)
 ....

Shopping for clothes

5 Reorder the conversation with the shop assistant.

a Over there? Thank you. ☐
b It's size 10. ☐
c Sure. The changing rooms are over there. ☐
d No, sorry. It's too tight. ☐
e Can I try it on? ☐
f Excuse me, what size is this mini-skirt? [1]
g Is it OK? ☐
h OK. You need a size 12. ☐

12 The man who steals Helen.

Film types

1 Match the two halves to make types of films.

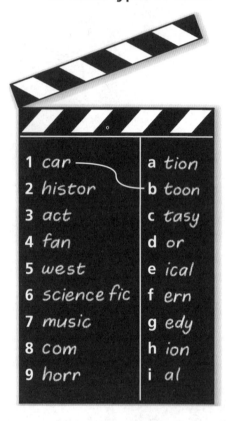

1 car —
2 histor
3 act
4 fan
5 west
6 science fic
7 music
8 com
9 horr

a tion
b toon
c tasy
d or
e ical
f ern
g edy
h ion
i al

1	b	2		3	
4		5		6	
7		8		9	

Relative pronouns: who, which and where

2a Complete the letter with *who*, *which* or *where*.

Dear Jo,

We've just come back from Los Angeles! It was great. One day we went to a café on Rodeo Drive ¹ ...where... all the film stars go. My friend had a chocolate milkshake ² .... cost $5! Then guess who we saw – Jennifer Aniston! She's the actress ³ .... was in the TV series 'Friends' and ⁴ .... is married to Brad Pitt. We went on a visit of the Stars' Homes and I saw the house ⁵ .... she and Brad live.

We also went to see a film in downtown LA called 'Hunter'. It's about a boy ⁶ .... makes friends with a lion cub but a hunter kills it in the end. It was good but I don't really like films ⁷ .... are sad.

Then we went to a restaurant ⁸ .... they had live music and I had a pizza ⁹ .... had ten big prawns on it. It was brilliant!

Write soon.
Best wishes
Max

2b Join the parts of the sentences with *who*, *which* or *where*.

1 The girl is Australian. She lives next door.
The girl who lives next door is Australian.

2 Where are the keys? They were on the table.
....
....

3 She found a good shop. They sell CDs there.
....
....

4 She wants to go to a park. She can ride her bike there.
....
....

5 The girl is called Camilla. She won first prize.
....
....

3a Complete the conversations.

1 A: *What type of film is 'Black Insect'?*

B: It's a horror film.
A: *What's it about?*
B: It's about a fly. The fly kills people when it touches them.

2 A: ....?
B: It's a western.
A: ....?
B: It's about a cowboy and an Apache Indian. They make friends.

3 A: ....?
B: It's a comedy.
A: ....?
B: It's about a school. The children take control.

4 A: ....?
B: It's an adventure film.
A: ....?
B: It's about a boy. The boy runs away from home.

3b Now write about the films.

1 *It's a horror film about a fly which kills people when it touches them.*

2 ....

3 ....

4 ....

Buying a cinema ticket

4 Complete the conversation about buying cinema tickets.

| six thirty   That's £12   my friend   ~~Can we have~~ |
| performance?   How old |

Ricky: ¹*Can we have* two tickets to see *Soldier On* please?

Girl: Which ² ....

Ricky: The ³ .... , please.

Girl: ⁴ .... are you?

Ricky: I'm fourteen and ⁵ .... 's thirteen.

Girl: That's OK. Right. ⁶ .... please.

13 Something important

Shapes and textures

1a Find the twelve words and write them in the squares. Then find mystery phrase number 13.

1 SH|ROUND|ARY — R O U N D
2 JUSOFTEUM
3 DRASMOOTHRAK
4 PROTHARDING
5 DISHINYOWD
6 BAROUGHANT
7 BIBENDYLAP
8 CORSMALLRUT
9 TRISQUARENTEC
10 TOTHICKLIE
11 HATHININE
12 PASTRAIGHTAL

13 The mystery phrase is ....

1b Match six of the words from 1a with the pictures.

1 *square*
2 ....
3 ....
4 ....
5 ....
6 ....

someone, something, somewhere; anyone, anything, anywhere; no one, nothing, nowhere

2 Complete the conversations.

a A: I hope there's [1] *something* valuable in that old box.
B: No, there isn't [2] *anything* valuable.
A: Are you sure?
B: Yes, I am. There's [3] *nothing* valuable at all.

b A: I hope there's [4] .... good to watch on TV this evening.
B: No, there isn't [5] .... good.
A: Are you sure?
B: Yes, I am. There's [6] .... good on all evening.

c A: I think that man is [7] .... famous.
B: No, he isn't [8] .... famous.
A: Are you sure?
B: Yes, I am. He's [9] .... famous at all.

d A: I hope you're going [10] .... nice on holiday.
B: No, we aren't going [11] .... nice.
A: Are you sure?
B: Yes, I am. There's [12] .... nice near here.

3 Complete the conversation. Choose one of the words from the box.

someone   something   somewhere
anyone.   ~~anything~~   anything   anywhere
no one   nothing.   nowhere

Sam: I'm bored. There isn't ¹ *anything* to do here in the summer and there's ² .... interesting to go.
Ricky: Perhaps there's ³ .... on TV.
Sam: No, there's ⁴ ....
Ricky: Are you sure?
Sam: Yes, I've just looked. There isn't ⁵ .... good on all evening. Anyway, it's only four o'clock.
Ricky: Let's find ⁶ .... to play football with.
Sam: There isn't ⁷ .... Believe me, there's ⁸ .... in town. They're all on holiday.
Ricky: Is there ⁹ .... near here where we can do some quad biking?
Sam: Yes, I think there's a quad bike course ¹⁰ .... near the swimming pool.
Ricky: Come on. Let's go!

4 Do the crossword.

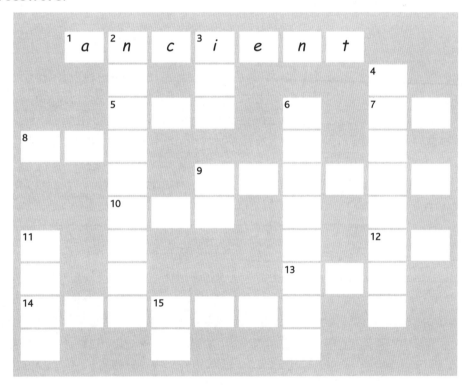

Across
1 I can speak modern Greek but not ...... Greek. (7)
5 I like vanilla ...... cream best. (3)
7 Look ...... this! It's an old bowl! (2)
8 Not small. (3)
9 You can see the Roman bowl in a ...... (6)
10 Good...... ! See you next week! (3)
12 I don't want to ...... late. (2)
13 Not well. (3)
14 Someone who gets into a house and steals something. (7)

Down
2 Someone who lives next door to you. (9)
3 Short form of 'I have'. (3)
4 Worth a lot of money. (8)
6 In our house, the sitting room is downstairs and the bedrooms are .... (8)
9 he/him; she/her; I/... (2)
11 Younger than a child. (4)
15 A: Where did you ...... yesterday?
   B: We went to see *Shrek 2*. (2)

14 Skills practice

New words
empire fierce fur
invade jewellery
Latin march
organised peaceful
smell (n) treasure

Reading

1 Read about the people. Match the texts with the pictures.

The Romans ☐   The Vikings ☐

Picture A

Picture B

THE ROMANS

The Romans had a very large empire from 44BC to 395AD. They came from Italy and they lived in different places in Europe. They arrived in Britain in 43AD. They built cities and roads, and taught people to speak Latin. They built large cities with big houses and public bath houses. They built straight roads so the army could march quickly from one place to another. The rich Romans lived and ate very well, but the poor Romans did not. They worked very hard. The Romans gave the English language Latin words like *medium* and *formula*.

THE VIKINGS

The Vikings came from Scandinavia: Sweden, Norway and Denmark. They invaded Britain and other countries in the north west of Europe from the eighth to the tenth centuries. They were very fierce people and fought bravely. Many of them stole food and treasure from the local people. Some Vikings were more peaceful. They sold furs and jewellery so they could buy other things. They needed their boats to travel around. Viking longships were thirty metres long, and were scary because they were full of fierce Vikings! The names for the days of the week in English come from the Viking words.

2 Complete the chart.

	Romans	Vikings
Where did they come from?	*Italy*	*Sweden, Norway and Denmark*
When did they come to Britain?		
What did they do in Britain?		
What words did they give to English?		

Listening

3 🎧 Listen to Ben and Emma talking about their visits to the Jorvik Museum and Verulamium Museum and note the correct place: Jorvik (J) or Verulamium (V).

Where is it?
1 York — J
2 St. Albans — ☐

What is there?
3 Large models — ☐
4 Coins and pots — ☐
5 A theatre — ☐
6 Sounds and smells — ☐

Writing tip
We use linkers (*so / because*) to join sentences.

Writing

4 Look at the texts in Exercise 1. Find the sentences which use the linkers *so* and *because*, and write them in your notebook.

5 Read Emma's postcard and then, in your notebook, write Ben's postcard about his visit to Jorvik.

> Dear Sue,
> I'm visiting Verulamium Museum with my class. It's in St. Albans so it's quite close to London. We're studying the Romans at school so my teacher decided to come here. I like the museum because it is near a Roman theatre.
> I hope you can visit it one day!
> Love from Emma

Dear Pete,
Jorvik Museum / with family. In York / quite a long way from / London. We study / Vikings / school / Mum and Dad / come here. I like / museum / has / sounds / smells.
Hope / you / visit / one day!
Best wishes,
Ben

Cartoon Time:
Clark and Lois – school reporters

6 Complete the conversation with the words in the box.

| doing | about | ~~some~~ | casual | so | bit |

Lois: Come on, Clark. You need ¹ *some* new clothes.
Clark: Good idea. I want something plain and ² ....

Lois: What ³ .... this flowery sweater, these spotted shorts and these orange sandals?
Clark: They're a ⁴ .... strange.
Lois: You're ⁵ .... old-fashioned. Try them on.

Clark: What are you ⁶ .... ?
Lois: I'm writing an article on boys who don't understand fashion. I need a photo.

15 Check — Lessons 11–14

1 Complete the sentences with *too* or *enough*, an adjective and the correct form of the verb *to be*.

1 I can't eat this ice cream – it 's too cold (cold).
2 This coffee .... (strong). Can I have some more milk?
3 This milk shake .... (sweet). Can I have some sugar?
4 This pizza .... (hot). I can't eat it!
5 Can I put some salt on these chips? They .... (salty).
6 My piece of cake .... (small). I want the large one!

Score ___ /5

2 Look at the pictures and write about the clothes.

1 a plain T-shirt
2 ....
3 ....
4 ....
5 ....
6 ....
7 ....
8 ....

Score ___ /7

3 Match the films with their definitions.

1 COMEDY — a a film which includes songs and often dancing
2 FANTASY — b a story about possible future events
3 HORROR FILM — c a film about an imaginary world and magic
4 MUSICAL — d a story about cowboys
5 SCIENCE FICTION — e a funny story which ends happily
6 WESTERN — f a film with frightening and unnatural things

1 e 2 ☐ 3 ☐ 4 ☐
5 ☐ 6 ☐

Score ___ /5

4 Match the phrases.

1 That's the assistant
2 Buckingham Palace is the place
3 That's the dog
4 Cathy is the hairdresser
5 I like the camp site
6 He bought the guitar

a where the Queen lives.
b who cut Brad Pitt's hair.
c where we go on holiday.
d which belonged to Madonna.
e who served me in the shop.
f which followed me home.

| 1 | e | 2 | | 3 | | 4 | |
| 5 | | 6 | |

Score ___ /5

5 Jemma is looking at a photograph album with her grandmother. Complete the sentences with *who*, *which* or *where*.

Grandmother:
1 Here's the house ___*where*___ I was born.
2 This is a tree _____ grew in our garden.
3 This is a picture of the Browns _____ lived next door.
4 Here's the village school _____ we all studied.
5 This is a picture of Mr Smith _____ taught us Maths.
6 And this is the park _____ we used to play.

Score ___ /5

6 Complete the sentences with the correct adjective.

1 Square tables are boring. Let's buy a r_ound_ one.
2 The new silver bowl is shiny but the old one is d_____ .
3 Country roads in England are quite b_____ but Roman roads are usually straight.
4 Do you like a soft bed or a h_____ bed?
5 It's cold so take a t_____ sweater. That one is too thin.
6 My mother always buys me smart clothes but I like c_____ things.

Score ___ /5

7 Complete the conversation with *something / someone / somewhere / anything / anyone / nothing / no one*.

Josh: Hi, Amy. Are you doing ¹___*anything*___ on Saturday?
Amy: No, ²_____ . Why?
Josh: I'm not doing ³_____ . Let's do ⁴_____ together.
Amy: Is ⁵_____ from school free?
Josh: No, ⁶_____ is at home. I think they're all away on holiday.
Amy: We can think about it and decide tomorrow. I'm sure we'll think of ⁷_____ to go and ⁸_____ to do! We may even find ⁹_____ else to join us!

Score ___ /8

CHECK YOUR SCORE!

TOTAL ___ /40

☐ Brilliant! (30–40)
☐ Good! (20–29)
☐ OK (10–19)

16 France have just scored.

Words to do with sports

1 Do the sports crossword.

Across

1 One man, two .... (3)
3 You need a sports ...... to carry your sports clothes in. (3)
4 What sports do you ...... ? (4)
6 ...... him! He mustn't score! (4)
9 The ...... is 2–1. (5)
11 That's the final .... It's the end of the game. (7)
12 I don't like football ...... rugby. (2)
13 The score was 15–3, but ...... it's 15–12. (3)
15 A: Who won?
   B: No one. It was a 1–1 .... (4)
17 We went home after the match. Where did you ...... ? (2)
18 France ...... England 3–0. (4)
19 You do this when you want to take the ball from a player in the other team. (6)

Down

1 Let's watch the football ...... on TV. (5)
2 Don't stand ...... ! I can't see! (2)
3 We're going to the match ...... car. (2)
5 We mustn't ...... this match. Its an important one. (4)
7 Don't keep the ball. ...... it to me! (4)
8 The Italian football ...... is very good. (4)
10 We've got some good players but ...... manager is hopeless! (3)
11 Past tense of *win*. (3)
12 ...... ! That hurt! (2)
14 It's a draw. The final score is ...... –1. (3)
15 How often ...... you play tennis? (2)
16 They are going to practise ...... day and all night. (3)
17 Short for Grand Tour. (2)

Past participle forms

2 Cross out the extra letter in each past participle form. The extra letters spell a new word.

	Past participle	Extra letters			Past participle	Extra letters
1	wo~~i~~n	won	i	8	fotund		
2	donne			9	beatein		
3	madet			10	coome		
4	loset			11	senen		
5	knorwn			12	beacome		
6	bonught			13	hald		
7	scoared						

The new word is ....

Present perfect simple with *just*

3 Complete the sentences. Use the correct form of the verbs in the box.

find	lose	see	~~buy~~	have
win	make			

1 *He has just bought* .... some jeans.
2 .... some money.
3 .... dinner.
4 .... his wallet.
5 .... a ghost.
6 .... a cake.
7 .... a prize.

Present perfect simple with *already* and *yet*

4a Look at the list and write the questions.

> Don't forget!
> 1 have a shower ✓
> 2 make your bed ✗
> 3 have breakfast ✓
> 4 do your homework ✗
> 5 tidy your room ✓
> 6 find your football socks ✓
> 7 phone Lucy ✗
> 8 buy a birthday card for Ricky ✓

1 *Have you had a shower yet?*
2 ....
3 ....
4 ....
5 ....
6 ....
7 ....
8 ....

4b Look at the list in 4a again, and write about Gina's day in your notebook.

1 *She's already had a shower.*
2 *She hasn't made her bed yet.*

33

17 Have you ever ... ?

Transport and travel

1 Join the jigsaw pieces to make words to do with travel and transport.

1 plat
2 lor
3 air
4 jour
5 har
6 tax
7 mo
8 scoo
9 cara
10 sta
11 fli
12 tr

a) i
b) ney
c) ped
d) ip
e) form
f) port
g) ght
h) bour
i) tion
j) ry
k) ter
l) van

1 e platform
2 ☐ ....
3 ☐ ....
4 ☐ ....
5 ☐ ....
6 ☐ ....
7 ☐ ....
8 ☐ ....
9 ☐ ....
10 ☐ ....
11 ☐ ....
12 ☐ ....

Verb forms

2 Write the verbs in the correct list in alphabetical order.

travelled, fly, ridden, drove, went, ~~was~~, ride, flown, travelled, ~~be~~, gone, ~~were~~, travel, flew, rode, drive, ~~been~~, go, driven

Infinitive	Past simple	Past participle
1 be	was/were	been
2		
3		
4		
5		
6		

Present perfect simple with *ever* and *never*

3a Write *ever* or *never* in the correct place in the sentences.

1 Have you ridden a camel? (*ever*)
   Have you ever ridden a camel?

2 He has travelled abroad. (*never*)
   ....

3 Have they gone first class? (*ever*)
   ....

4 She has been on a double-decker bus. (*never*)
   ....

5 Have you flown in a jumbo jet? (*ever*)
   ....

6 We have driven to Scotland. (*never*) – It's too far.
   ....

3b Rearrange the words to make sentences.

1 plane. I flown never a 've in
   I've never flown in a plane.

2 first Have ever you travelled class?
   ....

3 They abroad. never 've been
   ....

4 seen you ever camel? a Have
   ....

5 's driven sports car. a never He
   ....

6 on she a motorbike? ridden Has ever
   ....

Buying a train ticket

4 Complete the conversation at a station ticket office. Choose words from the box.

| leave   Platform   Single |
| ~~Can~~   That's   tickets |

Lucy: ¹ *Can* I have two ² .... to London, please?

Man: ³ .... or return?

Lucy: Return, please.

Man: ⁴ .... £30.00.

Lucy: When does the next train ⁵ .... ?

Man: At 12.05 from ⁶ .... Three.

Lucy: Thank you.

Present perfect and past simple

5 Complete the postcard. Write the correct form of the present perfect or the past simple.

Hi Lucy!
This is a postcard of the London Eye.
¹ *Have you ever been* (you / ever / be) on it?
It's really impressive. I ² .... (never / be) so high in the air before. We ³ .... (come) here on a double-decker bus. After the London Eye, we ⁴ .... (get on) a boat at Westminster Bridge and ⁵ .... (go) up the River Thames under all the bridges. I ⁶ .... (never / be) on the river before. There ⁷ .... (be) lots of exciting buildings to see.
See you soon.
Love from
Cathy

We've been here for an hour.

Present perfect simple with *for* and *since*

1a Complete the sentences with *for* or *since*.

1 I've been here in Barbados ..*since*.. Monday.
2 They've lived in Bristol ..*for*.. six years.
3 He's been in the USA .... two months.
4 You haven't had anything to eat .... breakfast.
5 Rosie hasn't been to school .... weeks.
6 She's played the piano .... she was four years old.
7 I've had my new bike .... three weeks.
8 Alex hasn't watched TV .... Sunday.

1b Read the sentences and answer the questions with *for* and *since*.

1 In May I started to wear glasses.
 It is now July.
 A: How long have you had glasses?
 B: I *'ve had glasses since May.*
  I've had glasses for two months.

2 My grandparents moved to Oxford in 1960.
 It is now 2005.
 A: How long have your grandparents lived in Oxford?
 B: They ....
 ....

3 On Monday Sarah had long hair.
 On Tuesday her hair was short.
 It is now Friday.
 A: How long has Sarah had short hair?
 B: She ....
 ....

4 Kevin met Sally on 1st January.
 It is now 31st July.
 A: How long has Kevin known Sally?
 B: He ....
 ....

5 We joined the queue at 6 pm. It is now 8 pm.
 A: How long have we been in the queue?
 B: We ....
 ....

2 Write sentences using the present perfect simple with *for* or *since*.

1 I / know / Rachel / many years.
 I've known Rachel for many years.

2 You / see / Beth / the weekend?
 Have you seen Beth since the weekend?

3 She / study Italian / three years.
 ....

4 We / not be / back to Italy / nine months.
 ....
 ....

5 They / live / in the USA / 2002.
 ....

6 I / not have / any chips / for two weeks.
 ....

7 he / work / in that pizza restaurant / he left school?
 ....
 ....

Types of book

3a Put in the missing vowels (a, e, i, o, u).

1	DTCTV STRY	detective story
2	FNTSY BK	....
3	GHST STRY	....
4	RMNTC NVL	....
5	SHT STRY	....
6	SCNC FCTN BK	....
7	DVNTR STRY	....
8	BGRPHY	....
9	HSTRCL NVL	....
10	FRY TL	....

3b What type of book do these sentences come from?

1 'When I came near, I saw that the woman in the white dress had no face.'
.a ghost story......................

2 'Once upon a time, there was a beautiful princess ...'
....

3 'I love you, Clarissa. I will always love you.'
....

4 'When I left home, I had no money and nowhere to go.'
....

5 'Detective Inspector Bates looked at the two keys.'
....

6 'Lady Jane smiled when she saw King Henry.'
....

7 'He left school in 1987 and started to work on the *Daily Star* newspaper.'
....

8 'It is the year 2090. Spaceship Enterprise has just landed on the Moon.'
....

4 Ricky and Gina are doing a school 'Readathon' to make money for a children's hospital. A reporter is interviewing them for the local newspaper. Complete the interview.

| done   called   for   How many   ~~Fine~~ |
| read   When   exaggerate   yet!   since |
| How often   just |

Reporter: Hello. How's the 'Readathon' going?

Ricky: ¹ *Fine* , thank you.

Reporter: What are you reading?

Ricky: I'm reading a book ² .... *The Chrysalids*. It's a science fiction story.

Reporter: ³ .... did the 'Readathon' start?

Ricky: On Monday.

Reporter: It's now Friday. ⁴ .... books have you read ⁵ .... Monday?

Ricky: I've ⁶ .... three.

Gina: Don't ⁷ .... , Ricky. You've only ⁸ .... started *The Chrysalids*. You haven't finished it ⁹ ....

Reporter: ¹⁰ .... does your school do this 'Readathon'?

Gina: Our school has ¹¹ .... it ¹² .... three years now.

Reporter: Great. I hope you enjoy the rest of your book, Ricky.

Skills practice

New words
comfortable
delicious   eagle
luxurious   passenger
symbol   twice

Reading

1 Read about the trains. Match the pictures with the texts.

Indian Pacific ☐   Ghan ☐

AUSTRALIAN TRAINS

Australia is a very large country. It takes a long time to drive in a car from one side to the other. People usually fly but they sometimes travel by train. Read about two of the train journeys which you can take across Australia.

INDIAN PACIFIC

The Indian Pacific railway runs between Perth and Sydney via Adelaide. It is called the Indian Pacific because it runs from the Indian Ocean in the west to the Pacific Ocean in the east. The journey is 4,352 kilometres long. Passengers spend three nights on board. Trains leave Perth twice a week, on Wednesdays and Sundays. The symbol of the train is an eagle.

GHAN

The Ghan railway was finished in 2004. It runs from Adelaide in the south to Darwin in the North, via Alice Springs. It is called the Ghan after the Afghan workers and their camels who helped to build the railways across Australia in the nineteenth century. The journey is 2,979 kilometres long. Passengers spend two nights on board. Trains leave Adelaide twice a week on Sundays and Fridays. The symbol of the train is a camel.

Picture A

Picture B

2a Look at the map and draw the routes which the trains follow.

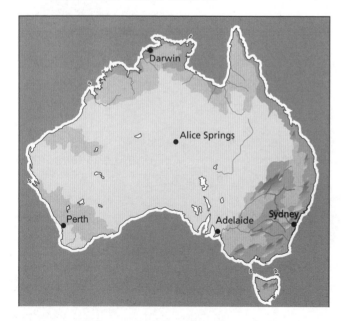

2b Complete the chart with information from the texts.

	Indian Pacific	Ghan
Where does the train run to and from?	*Perth / Sydney*	
Via where?		
Where and when does it leave?		
How far is the journey?		
How long do passengers spend on board?		
What is the symbol of the train?		

3 Read these sentences about the Orient Express train and try to guess the meaning of the numbered words. Then check the meanings in the box at the bottom of the page.

George Pullman

In 1864 a clever and ¹*innovative* man, George Pullman, built a train. It was very beautiful and ²*opulent*. The Pullman train ran from London to Brighton. It was ³*illuminated by electricity*. Later, George Pullman connected trains to ⁴*ferries* so people could travel by train from London to Paris.

Writing

4 Emma has written an essay about her journey on the Orient Express train. Complete her essay by filling in the gaps.

The most exciting journey I ¹ *have ever made* (ever / make) was on the Orient Express. We ² .... (travel) from London to Venice via Paris. The train ³ .... (be) very comfortable. We ⁴ .... (eat) delicious food, and we ⁵ .... (sleep) in special compartments. We ⁶ .... (see) the Alps. I ⁷ .... (enjoy) it very much and I ⁸ .... (be) sorry when we ⁹ .... (arrive) in Venice!

5 In your notebook, write about the most exciting journey you've ever made.

Portfolio

The most exciting journey I have ever made was ....

Meanings
innovative = introducing new ideas
opulent = luxurious
illuminated by electricity = had electric lights
ferries = boats which take passengers short distances

Cartoon Time:
Clark and Lois – school reporters

6 Complete the conversation with the words in the box.

| ages | ~~down~~ | chance | exaggerate |
| useless | on | win | just |

Dan: Hi, guys. Come and sit ¹ *down*.
Lois: Hi, Dan. Are you going to ² .... ?
Dan: No. The other team are brilliant and we're ³ .... It's 0–0.

Clark: Don't ⁴ .... , Dan.
Dan: We haven't won a game for ⁵ .... and we're not going to win today.
Lois: There's still a ⁶ ....
Dan: Dream ⁷ .... !

Lois: You've ⁸ .... scored the best goal that I've ever seen!

20 Check Lessons 16–19

1 Complete the dialogue with words from the box.

| beat   match.   score   ~~team~~ |
| tournament.   win |

Ricky: Are you coming to the cinema on Saturday afternoon, Sam?
Sam: No, I'm playing football. I'm in the school ¹ *team* and it's an important ² ....
Ricky: Why?
Sam: Well, we're playing in a ³ .... If we ⁴ .... the other schools on Saturday we'll ⁵ .... the cup!
Ricky: Do you enjoy playing?
Sam: Yes, I do when I ⁶ .... a goal!

Score ___ /5

2 Put the words in the correct order to make sentences.

1 just | goal. | a | scored | England | have
England have just scored a goal.

2 Troy. | already | seen | We | have
....

3 you | yet? | phoned | he | Has
....

4 aunt | My | given | me | just | has | £10.
....

5 homework | finished | you | yet? | Have | your
....

6 Sarah | not | has | her | tidied | yet. | room
....

Score ___ /5

3 Match the two halves to make complete sentences.

1 We had a lot of luggage so we took a
2 Visitors to London enjoy travelling on the red
3 When I was a child we used to go on holiday in a
4 Trains to Scotland leave from King's Cross
5 We got to the airport just in time for our
6 He hasn't got enough money for a car so he rides a

a station
b moped
c flight
d double-decker buses
e taxi
f caravan

| 1 | e | 2 | | 3 | | 4 | |
| 5 | | 6 | |

Score ___ /5

4 Ricky is showing his Italian friend Pietro around London. Complete the conversation with words from the box.

| ever   never   have.   ~~there~~   went |

Ricky: Look, ¹ *there* 's the London Eye.
Pietro: It's huge!
Ricky: Yes, it's enormous, isn't it?
Pietro: Have you ² .... been on it?
Ricky: Yes, I ³ .... We ⁴ .... on it last year.
Pietro: Was it exciting?
Ricky: Yes, but I've ⁵ .... been so terrified in my life!

Score ___ /4

5 Number the sentences in the correct order to make a conversation.

- [ ] a Return, please.
- [ ] b That's £43.00.
- [ ] c When does the next train leave?
- [ ] d Single or return?
- [ ] e Thank you!
- [1] f Can I have a ticket to York, please?
- [ ] g It leaves at 11.35 from Platform 6.

Score ___ /6

6 Write the questions and the answers.

1 How long / you / know / each other ?
   How long have you known each other?
2 We / know / each other / we / be / at school.
   ....
3 How long / you / play / the guitar, Don?
   ....
4 I / play / the guitar / eleven years old.
   ....
5 How long / Craig / play / the drums?
   ....
6 He / play / the drums / two years.
   ....
7 How long / you / be / in London?
   ....
8 We / be / in London / ten days.
   ....

Score ___ /7

7 Complete the sentences with *for* or *since*.

1 John's had toothache ___for___ two days.
2 We've lived in this house .... 1998.
3 Sandra has played tennis .... she was a child.
4 I've studied Spanish .... three months but I can't speak it yet!
5 My father has worked in London .... twenty-five years.
6 They've been friends .... they met at school.

Score ___ /5

8 Match the books with their definitions.

1 DETECTIVE STORY
2 GHOST STORY
3 BIOGRAPHY
4 FAIRY TALE

a a story about the spirit of a dead person
b an account of someone's life
c a story about imaginary magical people
d a story about a crime, often a murder

| 1 | d | 2 | |
| 3 | | 4 | |

Score ___ /3

CHECK YOUR SCORE!

TOTAL ___ /40

- [ ] Brilliant! (30–40)
- [ ] Good! (20–29)
- [ ] OK (10–19)

21 What will happen?

will / won't

1a Match the phrases. Then write the fortune-teller's predictions.

✓	✗
1 travel to Brazil	a marry her
2 get a job in a beach café	b leave the UK again
3 learn Spanish	c go by car
4 meet a beautiful girl	d stay in England
5 travel round Brazil by bus	e speak it very well
6 go back to the UK	f earn a lot of money

1 [d] *You'll travel to Brazil. You won't stay in England.*

2 ☐ ....

3 ☐ ....

4 ☐ ....

5 ☐ ....

6 ☐ ....

1b Complete the conversation with *'ll*, *will* or *won't*.

Sam: Where ¹ *will you* be in ten years' time?

Ricky: I'm sure I ² .... be back home in the USA. What about you?

Sam: No, I had a dream last night about the future. I ³ .... stay here in England. I ⁴ .... go to Australia.

Ricky: To Australia? What ⁵ .... you do there?

Sam: I ⁶ .... have a surfing school on Bondi Beach in Sydney.

Ricky: You ⁷ .... know anyone there.

Sam: That's OK. My friends ⁸ .... come and visit me every weekend because in ten years' time, planes ⁹ .... fly to Sydney in three hours. They ¹⁰ .... take all day to get there any more!

Ricky: Dream on!

Technology

2a Find ten words to do with computer technology.

```
K E Y B O A R D M
A N D I S C U R O
J T O N M R S A N
L A P T O P S F I
W R G E D L I M T
E S C R E E N O O
B C O N M N T U R
I B D E F K P S U
S O F T W A R E V
```

2b Complete the technology verbs.

1 to s *ur* f the internet
2 to c............t to the internet
3 to s............h the web
4 to d............d music
5 to s............d a text message
6 to r............e an email

3 Complete the conversation with *'ll*, *will* or *won't* and a verb from the box.

> disappear   surf   do?   ~~communicate~~
> happen   predict   replace   be
> send and receive

A: I bet you that in ten years' time people ¹*won't communicate* by letter any more.
B: What ² .... they ....
A: They ³ .... emails or text messages on their mobile phones.
B: But surely text messages ⁴ .... phone calls!
A: Yes, they will, because they're cheaper. In fact I think phone boxes ⁵ .... completely.
B: Maybe you're right.
A: I am right! And people ⁶ .... the Internet on their mobile phones too.
B: What ⁷ .... to computers?
A: There ⁸ .... a computer in every room of the house! And when you're in a bad mood, your computer ⁹ .... your mood and play the right sort of music.
B: Wow! I love technology!

4 Number the sentences in the correct order and say what Sam's dream robot will and won't do.

a shout at me or get angry. It will make ☐
b be any mistakes. It will be brilliant! ☐
c me in a fast car to school. After school it will ☐
d My dream Robot will wake me in ☐ *1*
e my breakfast and bring it to me ☐
f in bed. Then I will get dressed and it will drive ☐
g the morning and then five minutes later, it ☐
h do my homework and there won't ☐
i will check that I'm still awake. It won't ☐

22 I'll help you.

Furniture and furnishings

1a Find the missing letter for each piece of furniture.

| H | I | P | E̶ | F | B | L | C | U |

1 BD   ....BED....
2 RG   ....
3 SOA   ....
4 TABE   ....
5 BOOKASE ....
6 CUPOARD ....
7 ARMCAIR ....
8 COMUTER ....
9 TELEVSION ....

1b Write the words in the puzzle and find hidden word number 9.

The hidden word 9 is ....

will / won't for offers, promises and decisions

2a Look at the pictures and complete the words.

1 the s _hopping_ ....
2 the m ....
3 some s ....
4 the b ....
5 the f ....
6 the d ....
7 a t .... h
8 some c ....
9 some d ....
10 the p .... and g ....

Now use a verb from the box to write offers.

| make make buy d̶o̶ put put |
| move sort blow up borrow |

1 ...I'll do the shopping....................
2 ....
3 ....
4 ....
5 ....
6 ....
7 .... on the table.
8 ....
9 ....
10 .... on the table.

2b Circle the correct verb form.

1 Hmm. The table doesn't look very nice. I think *I'll put* / *I put* a tablecloth on it.
2 Don't worry about the music. *I bring* / *I'll bring* all your favourite CDs.
3 What time *do you come* / *are you coming* this evening?
4 A: Is Martha coming to the party?
   B: I don't know. *I'll phone* / *I phone* her now.
5 What *do you wear* / *are you wearing* for the party tonight?
6 On Fridays and Saturdays *I go to bed* / *I'm going to bed* at half past nine.
7 There's lots of time. *I buy* / *I'll buy* the drink this afternoon.
8 I hope *you're going to tidy* / *you're tidying* this room before you go to bed.
9 A: What would you like to drink?
   B: *I have* / *I'll have* a cola, please.

3 Write the responses to the reminders.

1 Remember to take away the rug.
   Yes, I will.
2 Don't forget to buy the cola.
   No, I won't.
3 Remember to buy some balloons.
   ....
4 Don't forget to move the furniture.
   ....
5 Don't forget to take away the lamp.
   ....
6 Remember to bring your CDs.
   ....
7 Don't forget to invite Harry and Emma.
   ....
8 Remember to clean the room after the party.
   ....

Offering and reminding

4 Number the sentences in the correct order. Lucy and Sam are going to stay with their grandmother for the weekend.

a OK. I'll go and get the car now. It's time to leave. ☐
b It's here. Now don't forget to help Gran in the kitchen. ☐
c Yes, we are. Where's Gran's present? ☐
d And remember to say 'thank you' when you leave on Sunday. ☐
e No, we won't. ☐
f Are you ready to go? [1]
g Yes, we will. I promise. We always say 'thank you'. ☐

23 I'd rather work outside.

Jobs

1 Look at the picture. Write the jobs in the word puzzle, and find the hidden job number 14.

The hidden job number **14** is ....

would like to

2 Write conversations with *would like to*.

1 **A:** (doctor?) *Would you like to be a doctor?*
   B: (vet) *No, I wouldn't, but I'd like to be a vet.*

2 **A:** (TV reporter?) ....
   B: (TV newsreader) ....

3 **A:** (hairdresser?) ....
   B: (model) ....

4 **A:** (police officer?) ....
   B: (firefighter) ....

5 **A:** (ski instructor?) ....
   B: (football coach) ....

6 **A:** (pilot?) ....
   B: (car driver) ....

46

would prefer to / would rather

3 Look at the pictures and write conversations with *would prefer to* and *would rather*.

1 (prefer / work indoors / outdoors)
   A: *Would you prefer to work indoors or outdoors?*
   B: *I'd prefer to work outdoors.*

2 (rather / work with people / with animals)
   A: *Would you rather work with people or work with animals?*
   B: *I'd rather work with animals.*

3 (prefer / work in one place / travel around)
   A: ....
   B: ....

4 (rather / start work early / finish work early)
   A: ....
   B: ....

5 (rather / work with computers / work in television)
   A: ....
   B: ....

6 (prefer / be a hairdresser / be a newsreader)
   A: ....
   B: ....

4 Complete the conversation using the words and phrases from the box.

> do   That's no surprise!   ~~would you like~~
> sounds   to work   What about you
> prefer   I'm not sure.   wouldn't   I'd like
> to be   Typical!   rather

Sam: What ¹ *would you like* to do when you leave school, Ricky?

Ricky: ² .... to work with computers.

Gina: ³ .... You're computer crazy!

Ricky: No, really. A job with computers ⁴ .... interesting.

Sam: Which would you ⁵ .... be, a computer engineer or a web designer?

Ricky: I'd ⁶ .... to be a web designer. They earn lots of money.

Gina: ⁷ ....

Ricky: Don't be so mean. Anyway, ⁸ .... , Lucy?

Lucy: Me? ⁹ .... I ¹⁰ .... like to work indoors all the time. That's too boring. I'd prefer ¹¹ .... outdoors. In fact I think I'd like ¹² .... a ski instructor. I love skiing.

Sam: But you can't ¹³ .... that every day!

24 Skills practice

New words
annoying   campaign
inform   informative
interrupt   interview (v)
necessary   take seriously

Reading

GOOD, BAD OR FUNNY?
We asked our readers what they think about advertisements on television.

Daisy, 14
I think advertisements are annoying. You've just started watching a programme and then the advertisements interrupt it. It drives me crazy! They're really boring and they're also a waste of time. Most of them are about cars, washing powder or cat food! I know they're necessary to pay for the programmes we want to watch, but I'd rather not have them.

Vince, 15
I think advertisements can be good. Some are useful. For example, healthy eating and safe driving campaigns are educational as well as informative. I think a lot of young people find them helpful, because they learn about things. They're no good if they are too shocking, though. People just switch off!

Sarah, 13
I think ads are great! My friends also really enjoy them. Sometimes they're better than the actual programmes. I like the funny ones, and ones that tell a story, too. I don't think people take them seriously. If they don't like them they can go and make a cup of tea! I'd like to write ads when I'm older. That would be a cool job.

1a Read the texts about advertisements on television and answer the questions.

Who thinks advertisements
1 are useful? ......Vince......
2 are enjoyable? ....
3 are annoying? ....
4 would be fun to write? ....
5 inform people? ....
6 pay for programmes? ....

1b Find the adjectives in the texts with positive and negative meanings.

Positive
1 g_ood_   5 h..........
2 u.......... 6 g..........
3 e.......... 7 f..........
4 i.......... 8 c..........

Negative
1 a..........
2 b..........
3 s..........

Listening

2 🎧 Listen to the interview. Complete the chart.

Programmes	Girls and Boys	Boys	Girls
Chat shows			
Comedy			
Documentaries			

Programmes	Girls and Boys	Boys	Girls
Films			
Music	✓		
Sports			

Writing tip

When we want to add information, we can use *too*, *also* and *as well as*.

3a Find examples of *too*, *also* and *as well as* in the texts in Exercise 1.

They're really boring and they're <u>also</u> a waste of time.

3b Join the sentences.

1. These shoes are nice. They're comfortable. (and / also)

   These shoes are nice, and they're also comfortable.

2. He's kind. He's clever. (and / too)

   ....

3. She's a good singer. She's a good dancer. (as well as)

   ....

Writing

4 Read Sarah's paragraph about her favourite television programme, then, in your notebook, write about your favourite programme.

> **My favourite programme**
>
> I like comedy programmes best. I love 'Friends' because it's interesting and funny too. The six characters are all kind and they're also clever. I think it's well-written as well as intelligent. My sister doesn't watch television very much. She plays games on her computer or surfs the Net. My brother likes sports programmes but I think they're boring. He also drives me crazy because he channel hops all the time!

My favourite programme
I like ... because ...

Cartoon Time:
Clark and Lois – school reporters

5 Complete the conversation with the words in the box.

| bet | Typical | Fine | door | sure | Don't |
| hand | ~~going~~ | Help | | | |

A
Happy Birthday Mum

Clark: How's it ¹ *going*, Lois?
Lois: ² .... , but this sofa is too heavy for me.
Clark: ³ .... worry. I'll give you a ⁴ ....
Lois: Thanks.

B

Lois: There's someone at the ⁵ .... I ⁶ .... it's my mum.
Clark: No. Don't go. ⁷ .... !

C
Happy Birthday Mum

Mum: Where's Clark?
Lois: I'm not ⁸ ....
Mum: Perhaps he's gone home..
Lois: ⁹ .... ! He's so lazy.

25 Check Lessons 21–24

1 Complete the email with *'ll* or *won't*.

Dear Alice,

I'm so excited! Next week I ¹ won't be in school. I ² .... be on holiday in Spain! My older brother and I are going there on Saturday but Mum and Dad ³ .... join us until Monday. So we ⁴ .... have two days by ourselves. The best thing is we ⁵ .... be able to do what we like. We ⁶ .... cook for two days – we ⁷ .... eat pizza and ice cream. We ⁸ .... sleep as long as we want. We ⁹ .... do any work.
I expect we ¹⁰ .... spend all our time in the swimming pool!

With love,

Tina

Score ___ /9

2 Label the computer.

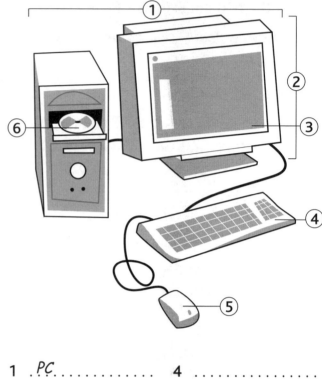

1 PC............ 4 ....
2 m .... 5 ....
3 .... 6 ....

Score ___ /5

3 Reorder the letters to make words.

1 teshc fo swrdare
chest of drawers

2 ushocin
....

3 plma
....

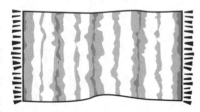
4 gru
....

5 rrroim
....

6 bedorraw
....

Score ___ /5

50

4 Complete with 'll or won't.

1 Now promise me you 'll......... be good.
2 We .... be good.
3 We .... eat too much food.
4 We .... spend all our money.
5 We .... get lost.
6 We .... come home at six o'clock.
7 We .... look after each other.

Score ___ /6

5 Write sentences.

1 Would she like to have tea or coffee? (prefer / tea)
   She'd prefer to have tea.
2 Would he like to eat spaghetti or pizza? (rather / pizza)
   ....
3 Would they like to go by bus or train? (prefer / train)
   ....
4 Would you like to see *Troy* or *Lord of the Rings*? (rather / *Troy*)
   ....
5 Would they like to visit Paris or Rome? (prefer / Rome)
   ....
6 Would you like to play tennis or football? (rather / tennis)
   ....

Score ___ /5

6 Make six sentences from the chart.

A firefighter	cuts	footballers
A hairdresser	trains	sick animals
A pilot	makes	fires
A vet	flies	things with wood
A football coach	fights	planes
A carpenter	helps	hair

1 *A firefighter fights fires.*
2 ....
3 ....
4 ....
5 ....
6 ....

Score ___ /5

7 Complete the sentences.

1 Would you rather be a doctor or a vet?
   I'd rather be a vet. because I like animals.
2 Would you prefer to be a teacher or a waiter?
   .... because I like children.
3 Would you prefer to be a hairdresser or an air hostess?
   .... because I don't like flying.
4 Would you prefer to be a model or a gardener?
   .... because I like being outside.
5 Would you rather be a detective or a pilot?
   .... because I love travelling.
6 Would you rather be a cook or a carpenter?
   .... because I love food.

Score ___ /5

CHECK YOUR SCORE!

TOTAL ___ /40

☐ Brilliant! (30–40)
☐ Good! (20–29)
☐ OK (10–19)

26 If I'm in a bad mood, ...

Zero conditional

1a Match the two halves to make complete sentences.

1 If my brother gets a bad mark
2 If one of her friends has a birthday
3 If my dad doesn't like a TV programme
4 If my sister is in a bad mood
5 If I invite friends home
6 If my brother stays late at a friend's house

a my brother plays loud music to annoy them.
b he doesn't tell Dad about it.
c she stays in her room.
d my mother gets angry with him.
e she always buys a big present.
f he switches the TV off.

| 1 | b | 2 | | 3 | | 4 | | 5 | | 6 | |

1b Match the pictures 1–6 with the cues a–f and write sentences.

1 my sister / get home late from school

2 I / want to go to the cinema

3 my brother / miss the bus

a I / ask my dad for some money
b Mum / not give me any pocket money
c Mum / get angry with her
d Dad / switch off his CD player
e he / walk home
f Kate / always / have the largest piece

4 we / have cake for tea

5 I / not tidy my room

6 Jack / play his rap music loudly

1 [c] *If my sister gets home late from school, Mum gets angry with her.*
2 ☐ ....
3 ☐ ....
4 ☐ ....
5 ☐ ....
6 ☐ ....

Personality adjectives

2 Complete the adjective and match it with its correct meaning.

1 S _H_ Y [f]
2 L _ _ Y ☐
3 R _ _ E ☐
4 F _ _ _ _ Y ☐
5 P _ _ _ _ _ E ☐
6 C _ _ _ _ _ R ☐
7 H _ _ _ _ _ _ L ☐
8 F _ _ _ _ _ _ _ Y ☐

a makes people laugh
b gets good marks at school
c likes helping other people
d not polite
e makes friends easily
f doesn't like meeting new people
g says 'please' and 'thank you'
h sits around and does nothing

3a Choose ten adjectives from the box to match the definitions.

> loyal   greedy   sensible
> moody   honest   ~~dishonest~~
> patient   impatient   annoying
> bad-tempered   generous
> mean   big-headed   modest
> easy-going   tidy   untidy

Someone who:
1 never tells the truth is _dishonest_.
2 always does the right thing is ....
3 hates waiting is ....
4 eats a lot is ....
5 talks about his or her good points is ....
6 never puts things back in the right place is ....
7 is sometimes in a good mood and sometimes in a bad mood is ....
8 never says a bad word about a friend is ....
9 often gets angry is ....
10 often makes people angry is ....

3b Write the opposites.

1 impatient
   patient
2 dishonest
   ....
3 untidy
   ....
4 bad-tempered
   ....
5 generous
   ....
6 big-headed
   ....

4 Complete the sentences.

> My Favourite Uncle
> My favourite uncle is Uncle Tommy. There are lots of reasons why:
> - He's always very ¹ _generous_. If it's my birthday, he always gives me some money or a nice present.
> - He's very ² .... If something goes wrong, he always knows what to do.
> - He's very ³ .... He knows the answer to everything!
> - He's got a brilliant job but he's never ⁴ .... about it. He's always very ⁵ ....
> - If I've got a problem with my homework, or with my bike, he's always very ⁶ ....
> - He's very ⁷ .... He always tells the truth.
> - My friends all like him because he's always very friendly and ⁸ .... In fact, we can do what we like in his flat.
> - He isn't perfect. In fact he's very ⁹ ...., like me! There are always lots of books and clothes everywhere in his flat. But that's why I like him!

53

27 If you do it quickly, ...

Cooking verbs

1a Complete the cooking verbs.

BANANA AND CHOCOLATE SURPRISE
(For 2 persons)
- ¹P _e e_ l two bananas.
- ²S _ _ _ _ e each banana into ten pieces.
- ³M _ _ _ t some dark chocolate. Be careful it doesn't ⁴b _ _ _ _ n!
- ⁵H _ _ _ t some cream but don't ⁶b _ _ l it.
- ⁷P _ _ _ r the cream into the chocolate.
- ⁸C _ _ _ p some nuts.
- ⁹S _ _ _ _ _ _ k the nuts into the chocolate and ¹⁰m _ _ well.
- ¹¹T _ _ _ t to see if it is sweet enough!
- ¹²P _ _ _ r the chocolate mixture over the bananas.
- ¹³S _ _ _ v immediately and enjoy!

Note
Some people like to ¹⁴f _ _ _ bananas in butter, others like to ¹⁵g _ _ _ _ _ l or ¹⁶b _ k them but I don't like to ¹⁷c _ _ _ k bananas at all. Fresh bananas are best!

1b Read the recipe again and number the pictures in the correct order.

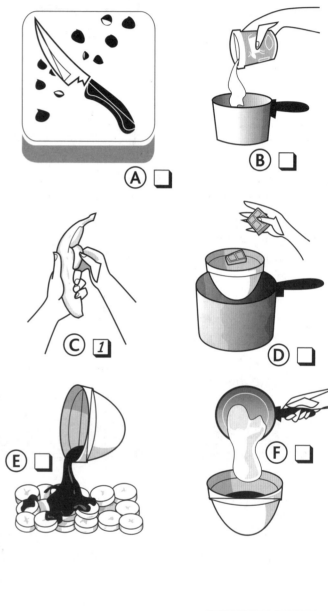

A ☐　B ☐

C 1　D ☐

E ☐　F ☐

G ☐

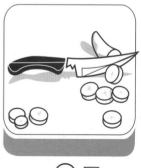

H ☐

First conditional

2a Circle the correct verb.

1 If we (don't)/ won't go now, we'll be late for school.
2 If they aren't home soon, we'll call / call the police.
3 It won't be so hot if you will sit / sit under the tree.
4 If I open / will open the window, the cat will jump out.
5 Mum gives / will give your hamburger to the dog if you don't want it.
6 If Jack asks / will ask for your telephone number, I won't give it to him.
7 She won't be tired at school tomorrow if she goes / will go to bed now.
8 If he calls again, I don't / won't answer the phone.

2b Complete the sentences using the two verbs in brackets.

1 If I ….. pass ….. my exams, Dad ….. will buy ….. me a CD player. (pass // buy)
2 My mum …………… you at the station if you …………… us when you're arriving. (meet // tell)
3 If I …………… at four o'clock, …………… home from school? (come // your brother / be)
4 If I …………… this exercise now, I …………… any homework to do. (finish // not have)
5 If you …………… hard, you …………… a good mark. (work // get)
6 If I …………… this letter to the USA today, …………… before Friday? (send // it / arrive)
7 If Mark …………… , I …………… him an email. (not phone // send)
8 She …………… the train if she …………… . (miss // not hurry)
9 …………… angry if you …………… your piano exam? (your parents / be // not pass)

3 Complete the note for Sam and Lucy from their mother. Use the correct form of the verbs in the box.

not/watch   find
burn.   ~~use~~   leave
be   not/finish
not/be   not/be
melt   need

Sam/Lucy!
I'm having tea with Mrs Hall next door. If you're hungry, make an omelette but please don't use all the eggs. If you ¹ ….. use ….. all of them, there ² …………… any for breakfast tomorrow. If you're making toast, remember to be careful. If you ³ …………… the toast, it ⁴ …………… . There's ice cream in the freezer, but put it back if you ⁵ …………… it. It ⁶ …………… if you ⁷ …………… it out on the kitchen table. And one last thing – please clear up after you! If I ⁸ …………… the kitchen in a mess, I ⁹ …………… pleased! If you ¹⁰ …………… me, I ¹¹ …………… at Mrs Hall's house.
See you later,
Mum

28 It may wake up!

Phrasal verbs

1a Circle the correct word.

1 I'm going to take *off* / *away* my sweater. I'm baking!
2 Let's turn *off* / *on* the light. I can't see.
3 What time do you wake *up* / *down* in the morning?
4 Please put *off* / *down* your pens. That's the end of the exam.
5 We're nearly there. We get *on* / *off* the bus at the next stop.
6 Can you pick *on* / *up* that piece of paper on the floor, please?
7 I hope you didn't throw *away* / *off* your bus ticket.
8 Put *up* / *on* your anoraks, please. It's going to rain.
9 Here are our tickets. Let's get *on* / *up* the train.
10 Can you turn *on* / *off* the TV? This programme is awful.

1b Complete the sentences with a phrasal verb.

1 Can you tidy your room, please, and ...*pick up*... your clothes from the floor.
2 Why don't you .... your new skirt? It's really nice.
3 Don't forget to buy a ticket before you .... the train.
4 I always .... when my dad gets up in the morning.
5 Let's .... the TV. *Friends* starts in five minutes.
6 I want to .... this wet T-shirt. It's horrible.
7 Don't .... those grapes. They're OK.
8 Remember to .... the light when you go to bed.
9 Do we .... the bus here or at the next stop?
10 I can't .... this book. It's so exciting.

First conditional with *when*

2a Circle the correct answer.

1 When I ...... school, I'll go to the USA. a will leave b (leave) c am leaving
2 I ...... you your homework when you stop talking. a give b 'll give c am giving
3 When the water ...... , I'll make the tea. a will boil b boiled c boils
4 When Max arrives, we ...... 'Happy Birthday'. a 'll sing b sang c sing
5 I'll tell him the news when he .... a wake up b wakes up c will wake up
6 Dad ...... a photo of you when the rain stops. a takes b is taking c will take

2b Complete the sentences.

1 It *'ll be* (be) spooky when they *turn off* (turn off) the lights.
2 When we .... (finish) our exams, we .... (have) a sleepover party.
3 He .... (phone) us when he .... (arrive).
4 I .... (talk) to you when there .... (not / be) anyone here.
5 When you .... (be) all ready, we .... (start) to build the pyramid.
6 When she .... (wake up) tomorrow, she .... (be) hungry.

Asking permission

3 Complete the dialogue with a word or phrase from the box.

```
can we   may   all right if   I'm sorry.
Excuse me.   may be   I'm afraid
no problem!
```

Gina: ¹ *Excuse me.* Is it ² .... we put our stuff over here?

Man: Yes, ³ .... But put it inside because it ⁴ .... rain.

Gina: OK. And ⁵ .... buy a can of cola? We're baking.

Man: No, ⁶ .... ⁷ .... you can't. The camp shop isn't open.

Woman: It's all right. There ⁸ .... some in the fridge. You look very hot!

may

4 Gina is packing her bag for a camping holiday. What is she taking? Match the two halves and write sentences with *may*.

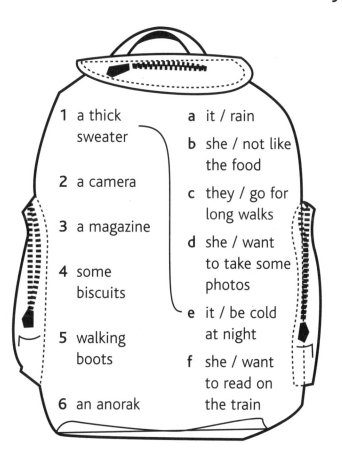

1 a thick sweater
2 a camera
3 a magazine
4 some biscuits
5 walking boots
6 an anorak

a it / rain
b she / not like the food
c they / go for long walks
d she / want to take some photos
e it / be cold at night
f she / want to read on the train

1 [e] *She's taking a thick sweater because it may be cold at night.*
2 [ ] ....
3 [ ] ....
4 [ ] ....
5 [ ] ....
6 [ ] ....

29 Skills practice

New words
announce   beep (v)   entry
recognise   spelling

Reading

BEST YOUNG INVENTOR

Here are the entries for our competition for young inventors. Which one do you think is best? We will announce the winner next month!

I have designed a Schoolwork Robot to help me in class. If I give my schoolwork to my robot it will tell me if my answer is right or not. It will also give me the correct spelling for words. The best thing is that it looks like a schoolbook so nobody knows that I've got it!
(Macey, 13 years)

I have invented a Super Skateboard. It will go faster if you push down with your right foot and it will go slower if you push down with your left foot. It turns left if you wave your left arm, and it goes right if you wave your right arm. It has a remote control so you can open doors and gates. It recognises my feet so it will only work if I use it.
(Harvey, 15 years)

My machine is a Cooking Fridge. It has a screen like a computer where you write the food you want. It tells you what is in the fridge and what meals it can make. When you decide what you want, the Cooking Fridge cooks it for you. You can programme it so it has your supper ready when you get home from school.
(Walter, 11 years)

My invention is a Teacher / Parent Alarm. If it hears a teacher coming it will beep so you can be good. It will also beep if it hears your parents coming. It's quite small so you can keep it in your pocket. I think it will be very useful!
(Harry, 12 years)

1 Read about the competition for best young inventor and answer the questions.

Which invention
1 has a remote control?
   the Super Skateboard
2 gives the correct spelling?
   ....
3 can you keep in your pocket?
   ....
4 cooks your supper?
   ....
5 beeps?
   ....
6 looks like a book?
   ....
7 has a screen like a computer?
   ....
8 recognises your feet?
   ....

2 Match the sentences.

1 If you say something to the robot
2 If you push down with your right foot
3 If it hears a teacher coming
4 When you decide what you want

a it cooks it for you.
b it will beep very loudly.
c it will tell you if your answer is right.
d it will go faster.

| 1 | c | 2 | | 3 | | 4 | |

58

Study tip

Do you remember how to improve your speaking?

3 Complete the sentences with words from the box.

| aloud clearly. discussion Emphasise |
| Listen mistakes. shy. ~~Speak~~ |

1 ...Speak... English as often as possible.
2 Don't be ....
3 Speak ....
4 .... the important words.
5 Don't be afraid to make ....
6 Practise reading dialogues .... when you are alone.
7 .... to other people speaking English.
8 Before a ...., make notes to help you.

Writing

4 Read this entry for the Best Young Inventor competition, then write about your invention in your notebook. Don't forget to draw it, too!

> My invention is called the Pick Up Robot.
>
> It is designed to pick up things from the floor quickly and easily.
>
> It looks like a spider with very long arms.
>
> The best thing is that your mum will stop telling you to tidy your room!

My invention is called ....
It is designed to ....
It looks like ....
The best thing is ....

Cartoon Time:
Clark and Lois – school reporters

5 Complete the conversation with the words in the box.

| whole ~~Gosh~~ right time least |
| baking mood |

Clark: ¹ ...Gosh... ! This sandwich is at ² .... two days old.
Lois: Let's write an article about the bad food here.
Clark: Good idea. On the ³ ...., the food is terrible.

Clark: Is it all ⁴ .... if we ask the cook some questions?
Woman: I doubt it! He's in a bad ⁵ ....

Woman: There he is. He's angry all the ⁶ ....
Lois: Err, I'm ⁷ .... I'm going outside.
Clarke: Me too!

59

30 Check Lessons 26–29

1 Lucy is talking about her holiday. Rewrite the sentences with *if* in the correct place.

1 I lie in the sun for too long / I get burnt.
   If I lie in the sun for too long I get burnt.

2 we go swimming / the weather's hot.
   ....

3 I beat my brother at tennis / he gets cross.
   ....

4 it's raining / we visit a museum.
   ....

5 I buy everyone an ice cream / I have enough money.
   ....

Score ___ /4

2 Choose the correct adjective.

1 She's very *loyal* / *moody*. You never know if she'll be happy or miserable.
2 He always knows the right thing to do. He's very *sensible* / *bad-tempered*.
3 I trust her completely – she's very *honest* / *big-headed*.
4 He's so *greedy* / *modest* – he won first prize at school but never told us.
5 Our teacher answers all our questions – she's very *patient* / *mean*.
6 If you keep your room *easy-going* / *tidy* you'll be able to find things!

Score ___ /5

3 Complete the sentences.

1 If I / have / enough money / I / buy / some CDs.
   If I have enough money I'll buy some CDs.

2 If we / visit / New York / I / practise my English.
   ....

3 I / not / pass / my exams / if I / not / work hard.
   ....

4 If it / be / good weather / we / have / barbecue / tomorrow.
   ....

5 We / not / see / the start of the film / if we / be / late.
   ....

6 If Danny / not / can / come / to the concert / I / ask / Laura.
   ....

Score ___ /5

4 Find nine cooking words.

P	X	C	H	O	P	M	I	S
G	E	P	M	I	X	N	L	P
B	A	K	E	O	J	K	W	I
S	L	I	C	E	N	U	C	U
A	L	B	E	A	T	K	S	M
F	S	J	H	E	A	T	P	F
R	P	L	G	M	E	L	T	B
P	B	O	I	L	V	O	M	N
Y	V	P	E	E	L	C	L	D

Score ___ /8

60

5 Alan has forgotten what his mother said. Can you help him? Match the sentences.

1 Get up — d
2 Turn off
3 Pick up
4 Throw away
5 Put on
6 Get on

a your clean clothes.
b the train.
c the television.
d at seven o'clock.
e your dirty clothes.
f your rubbish.

| 1 | d | 2 | | 3 | | 4 | |
| 5 | | 6 | |

Score ___ /5

6 Write sensible sentences.

1 I'll go to bed when I'm thirsty.
2 I'll eat my supper when it's a mess.
3 I'll wash my hair when I'm tired.
4 I'll tidy my room when I'm cold.
5 I'll wear my coat when I'm hungry.
6 I'll have a drink when it's dirty.

1 I'll go to bed when I'm tired.
2 ....
3 ....
4 ....
5 ....
6 ....

Score ___ /5

7 Complete the text with the correct phrasal verbs in the correct tense.

get off   get on   ~~get up~~   look at   pick up
put on   throw away   turn off   turn on

Tuesday 25th October

Yesterday I ¹ ...got up... early.
I ² .... my alarm clock,
³ .... the light and went to the bathroom. I washed and ⁴ .... my clothes.
I ⁵ .... my bag and ran to the bus. When I ⁶ .... the bus it was empty. I realised it was dark outside. I ⁷ .... my watch. It was five o'clock in the morning. I was very cross.
I ⁸ .... the bus, walked home and ⁹ .... my alarm clock!

Score ___ /8

CHECK YOUR SCORE!

TOTAL ___ /40

☐ Brilliant! (30–40)
☐ Good! (20–29)
☐ OK (10–19)

You don't have to ...

Sports places

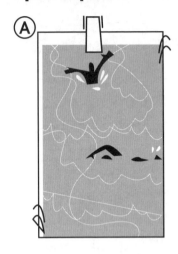
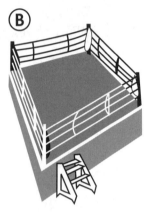

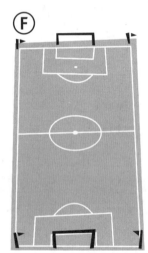

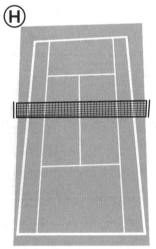

1 Complete the names of the sports places. Then write in the crossword the words which are circled.

A s *wimming*   (p *ool*)   = 1 across
B b _____ (r _____) = 3 across
C a _____ (t _____) = 5 across
D i _____ (r _____) = 7 across
E s _____ (p _____) = 1 down
F f _____ (p _____) = 2 down
G (g _____) c _____ = 4 down
H t _____ (c _____) = 6 down

must and mustn't

2 Circle *must* or *mustn't* in the sentences.

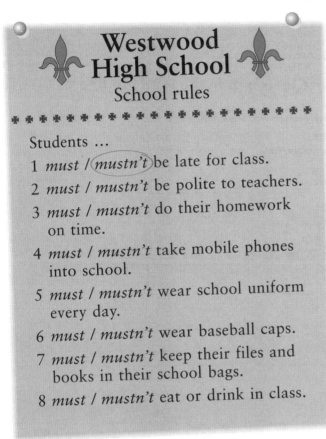

Westwood High School
School rules

Students …
1 must / *mustn't* be late for class.
2 must / mustn't be polite to teachers.
3 must / mustn't do their homework on time.
4 must / mustn't take mobile phones into school.
5 must / mustn't wear school uniform every day.
6 must / mustn't wear baseball caps.
7 must / mustn't keep their files and books in their school bags.
8 must / mustn't eat or drink in class.

have to

3a Write questions with the correct form of *have to* and one of the verbs.

| have | pay | ~~wear~~ | wear | bring | be |

1 A: ......Do I have to wear...... trainers?
  B: Yes, you do.
2 A: .... a member?
  B: Yes, she does.
3 A: .... an entrance fee?
  B: Yes, they do.
4 A: .... a swimming cap?
  B: No, I don't.
5 A: .... a shower before they swim?
  B: Yes, they do.
6 A: .... a towel?
  B: No, he doesn't.

3b In your notebook, write full answers to the questions in Exercise 3a.
1 *Yes, you have to wear trainers.*
2 *Yes, she* ....

mustn't, have to, don't have to

4 Complete the information for members of a tennis club with *mustn't*, *have to* or *don't have to*.

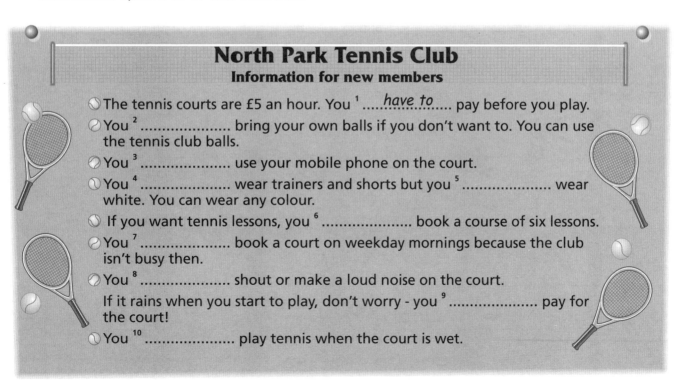

North Park Tennis Club
Information for new members

- The tennis courts are £5 an hour. You ¹......have to...... pay before you play.
- You ²................... bring your own balls if you don't want to. You can use the tennis club balls.
- You ³................... use your mobile phone on the court.
- You ⁴................... wear trainers and shorts but you ⁵................... wear white. You can wear any colour.
- If you want tennis lessons, you ⁶................... book a course of six lessons.
- You ⁷................... book a court on weekday mornings because the club isn't busy then.
- You ⁸................... shout or make a loud noise on the court.
- If it rains when you start to play, don't worry - you ⁹................... pay for the court!
- You ¹⁰................... play tennis when the court is wet.

You shouldn't cycle …

Common illnesses

1 Unscramble the letters of six illnesses and write the words in the puzzle to find the hidden word number 7.

1 A D H A C E H E
2 D L O C
3 C H U G O
4 A R E T T O S H O R
5 C H A M O T H A C E S
6 R A M P E T U R E E T

The hidden word number 7 is ……………………

have got + illnesses

2 Write questions and complete the answers.

1 A: What's the matter with him?
   B: He's ……got…… a ……cough…… .

2 A: ………………………………………
   B: ……………… got a ……………… and a s…………… t……………… .

3 A: ………………………………………
   B: ……………………… a ……………… .

4 A: ………………………………………
   B: ……………… a h……………… and a t……………… .

should and shouldn't

3 Give advice. Complete the sentences with *should* or *shouldn't*.

1. *You should* take some vitamin tablets.
2. .... go swimming.
3. .... go to bed late.
4. .... stay at home.
5. .... wear something warm.
6. .... go out without a jacket.
7. .... play football in the rain.
8. .... see a doctor.
9. .... lie down.
10. .... go to any parties.

I've got a bad cold and a temperature.

Visiting a doctor

4 Complete the conversation.

> medicine.   got   I see.   just to be sure.
> feel   a bit worried   ~~with~~   swimming
> see me   a few   cough   Maybe
> since   Thank you

Dr Chua: Good morning, Lucy. Now what's the matter ¹ *with* you?

Lucy: I've ² .... a cold and a bad ³ .... , Dr Chua.

Mrs Blake: I'm ⁴ .... about her. She's had it ⁵ .... Monday.

Dr Chua: ⁶ .... Well, Lucy. I'll give you some cough ⁷ ....

Lucy: Great. ⁸ .... , Dr Chua.

Dr Chua: But you should stay at home for ⁹ .... days.

Lucy: Oh! There's a ¹⁰ .... competition tomorrow and it's important!

Dr Chua: ¹¹ .... it is, but you shouldn't go swimming if you aren't well. In fact, you shouldn't go swimming for another week, ¹² ....

Lucy: All right.

Dr Chua: Come back and ¹³ .... if you don't ¹⁴ .... better next week.

33 What would you do?

Second conditional

1a Match the two halves. Then write full sentences with the correct form of the verb in brackets.

1 If I lived in the country,
2 If he won a million pounds,
3 If she ate all that ice cream,
4 If they wanted to come,
5 If she had the chance,
6 If you did your homework on time,

a she (have) a stomach ache.
b your teacher (not get) angry.
c I (get) a mountain bike.
d she (study) in the USA.
e he (not spend) any of it.
f they (phone) us.

1 [c]. *If I lived in the country, I'd get a mountain bike.*
2 ☐ ....
3 ☐ ....
4 ☐ ....
5 ☐ ....
6 ☐ ....

1b Write questions and answers with *if* and the second conditional. Choose the answers from the box.

> a lot of computer games
> chips, ice cream and bananas
> a Harry Potter book   Australia
> ~~my laptop~~   card games

1 What / save first / your house (be) on fire?
2 What / buy / your parents (give) you £100?
3 What games / play / you (not have) a TV or a computer?
4 What country / visit / you (have) a year's holiday?
5 What book / take / you (go) on a long train journey?
6 What food / eat / you (not like) fish or meat?

1 A: *What would you save first if your house was on fire?*
   B: *I'd save my laptop.*
2 A: ....
   B: ....
3 A: ....
   B: ....
4 A: ....
   B: ....
5 A: ....
   B: ....
6 A: ....
   B: ....

might

2 Complete the conversation with the correct form of the verbs. Use *might*, *'d*, *would* or *wouldn't* where appropriate.

Gina: If you won this competition, who ¹ *would you invite* (you / invite) to dinner?
Lucy: I don't know. I ² .... (ask) Justin Timberlake. He's cool.
Gina: Where ³ .... (you / go) to eat?
Lucy: I ⁴ .... (definitely / take) him to a Mexican restaurant. I love Mexican food.
Gina: But he ⁵ .... (not like) it! And if he didn't like it, he ⁶ .... (go) home. It's possible!
Lucy: I'm sure he ⁷ .... (not / do) that.
Gina: Anyway, where ⁸ .... (you / go) after the meal?
Lucy: I'm not sure. We ⁹ .... (go) to a disco, or maybe the cinema. But one thing is certain. He ¹⁰ .... (have) a brilliant evening with me!

Adjectives with prepositions

3a Choose words from the box to complete the newspaper article.

| interested good fond keen ~~mad~~ bored scared proud |

MARIA SHARAPOVA –
– TENNIS STAR OF TOMORROW?

Maria Sharapova was born in Russia in 1987. She has always been ¹ *mad* about tennis. When she was six, she played against a wall for hours every day and was never ² .... with it. She wasn't ³ .... on school subjects but she was ⁴ .... at tennis.

When she was seven, the family moved to Florida in the USA and met Nick Bolletieri, the director of the famous Bolletieri Tennis Academy. He was an important man, and Maria was a bit ⁵ .... of him! When he saw her play, he was immediately ⁶ .... in her and gave her a place at the Academy. Over the next few years, she won many matches and tournaments. When she won the ladies singles title at Wimbledon in the UK in 2004, her parents were very ⁷ .... of her. Today she lives in the USA but she is still ⁸ .... of her home country, Russia, and often goes back to visit.

3b Rewrite the sentences using one of the adjective phrases from Exercise 3a.

1 She likes her grandmother a lot.
   She's fond of her grandmother.

2 I don't like rap very much.
   ....
   ....

3 I really love skateboarding. I do it every minute of the day.
   ....
   ....

4 She thinks dogs are scary.
   ....
   ....

5 She can do Maths quite easily.
   ....
   ....

6 They think their daughter is fantastic.
   ....
   ....

34 Skills practice

New words
category   celebration
complicated   guidance
law   vary

Reading

WHEN ARE YOU A GROWN-UP?

Sally: Australia

In Australia the law says that young people are adults at eighteen. That's when we can buy alcohol and when we have to vote. In Australia we must vote when we are adults. It's the law. We can drive at seventeen and get married at sixteen if our parents agree. The strange thing is that we can leave school at fourteen years and nine months but we have to wait until we are fifteen before we can start work.

Ned: USA

In the United States, you can vote at eighteen, but you can't buy alcohol until you're twenty-one. In most states you can drive at sixteen. The age you can do other things is different from state to state. It's very complicated! In some states, for example Alaska, you can leave school at sixteen, but in others, like Arkansas, you have to stay at school until you're eighteen. The age you can get married is also different in different states. In most states you can marry at sixteen if your parents agree. In a few states, like California, you can get married at any age if your parents say it's OK!

Keiko: Japan

In Japan, we are adults at twenty. We have special celebrations then. At that age we can vote and buy alcohol. We can leave school at fifteen and drive at eighteen. Girls can get married at sixteen but boys have to wait until they're eighteen.

1 Read what these young people say about life in their countries and complete the chart.

	Australia	United States	Japan
Leave school	14 years and 9 months		
Drive a car			
Buy alcohol			
Get married			
Vote			

2 Answer the questions.

1 Where can you leave school at fifteen?
   in Japan
2 Where can you drive a car at sixteen?
   ....
3 Where do you have to be twenty before you can vote? ....
4 Where do you have to vote when you are an adult? ....
5 Where do you have to be twenty-one before you can buy alcohol?
   ....
6 Where can you get married at any age if your parents agree? ....

Listening

3 🎧 Listen to Fraser talking to his friend Pierre about films in Britain. Complete the chart.

BBFC film category	Who can see it?
U	Everyone
PG	
12A	
15	
18	

4 Match the things you need to check in your work with the examples.

1 spelling
2 grammar
3 word order
4 punctuation
5 handwriting

a capital letters at the beginning of sentences
b *i* before *e* except after *c*
c correct verb tenses
d Is it clear?
e adjectives before nouns

| 1 | b | 2 | | 3 | | 4 | | 5 | |

Writing

5 This paragraph has twelve mistakes. Check it and rewrite it correctly in your notebook.

In the UK the law says that young people are adults at eighteen. That has *is* when we can vote, by alcohol and get married. If our parents agrees, we can get marry younger, at sixteen. We can leaf school at sixteen and start to drive at seventeen. my grandmother say that when she were yung, she not become an adult until she had twenty-one, so young people in the past had to wait another three year before they were adults!

Cartoon Time:
Clark and Lois – school reporters

6 Complete the conversation with the words in the box.

worried   What   see   ~~matter~~   sure   fact   all

Lois: What's the ¹*matter* with you?
Clark: I hurt my finger, that's ² ....
Lois: I ³ ....

Lois: That could be dangerous. I'm a bit ⁴ .... I'm going to put a bandage on it, just to be ⁵ ....

Lois: ⁶ .... a hot day! In ⁷ .... , I'm going to swim in the river. Are you coming?

35 Check — Lessons 31–34

1 Complete the text with the correct words.

> course. court pitch ~~pool~~ rink track.

WESTMORE SPORTS CENTRE

The new Westmore Sports Centre has a large swimming ¹ _pool_.
There is a football ² .... and an athletics ³ ....
Six tennis ⁴ ....s have just opened.
An ice skating ⁵ .... will open next year.
There will also be a golf ⁶ ....

Score ___ /5

2 Lorna is talking about the rules at the Westmore Sports Centre. Write sentences with must or mustn't.

1 You / smoke / in the centre.
   You mustn't smoke in the centre.
2 You / chew gum / in the centre.
   ....
3 You / book / tennis courts / at the weekend.
   ....
4 You / take food or drink / into the pool.
   ....
5 You / shower / before / you / swim.
   ....

6 You / jump / in the pool.
   ....
7 You / use / a mobile phone.
   ....
8 Of course / you / be / a member!
   ....

Score ___ /7

3 Sam is looking after his Aunt Mary's dog, Rex. Aunt Mary has left him instructions. Complete the sentences with must, mustn't or don't have to.

> Instructions as follows:
> 1 Feed him at 5 o'clock.
> 2 Take him for a walk but only if you want to.
> 3 I don't want Rex to sleep on the bed!
> 4 Put his bed in the kitchen.
> 5 You don't need to bath him.

1 He _must_ feed him at 5 o'clock.
2 He .... take him for a walk.
3 Rex .... sleep on the bed.
4 He .... put his bed in the kitchen.
5 He .... bath him.

Score ___ /4

4 Write the words.

1 d l c o
   cold
2 g c u h o c
   ....
3 e e d a a h h c h
   ....
4 a a o e h h t s c c m s   a
   ....
5 e t p r t u a e e r m t
   ....

Score ___ /4

70

5 Match the advice with the problems and write the sentences.

a go to bed.
b read a book.
c practise more.
d ask your teacher.
e take an aspirin.
f go to the dentist.

1 [e] *You should take an aspirin.*
2 [ ] ....
3 [ ] ....
4 [ ] ....
5 [ ] ....
6 [ ] ....

Score ___ /5

6 Match the sentences.

1 If I had £100
2 If I studied harder
3 If I met Brad Pitt
4 If I had a television
5 If I were older
6 If I had a computer

a I could watch the Olympics.
b I'd buy some new shoes.
c I could go to the disco.
d I could surf the Internet.
e I'd do better at school.
f I wouldn't know what to say!

1 b 2 ___ 3 ___ 4 ___ 5 ___ 6 ___

Score ___ /5

7 Write sentences.

1 If Jane / win £1,000 / she / travel / round the world.
   If Jane won £1,000 she'd travel round the world.

2 Sid / pass / his exams / if he / work harder.
   ....

3 Bob / buy / a car / if he / know / how to drive.
   ....

4 If Jenny / organise / a party / she / invite all her friends.
   ....

5 Susie / make / a cake / if she / have time.
   ....

6 If Ron / play / football / well / he / be / in the team.
   ....

Score ___ /5

8 Complete the sentences with a preposition from the box.

| about at ~~in~~ of on with |

1 I'm not really very interested ...*in*... politics.
2 William's not very keen .... jazz. He prefers rap.
3 I'm really bored .... this programme. Shall we change channels?
4 Amy's absolutely mad .... Brad Pitt. She's seen all his films.
5 I don't like the dark. I'm really scared .... ghosts!
6 Josh is really good .... Maths. He always gets top marks.

Score ___ /5

CHECK YOUR SCORE!

TOTAL ___ /40

☐ Brilliant! (30–40)
☐ Good! (20–29)
☐ OK (10–19)

71

36 It's recycled.

The present simple passive

1 Rewrite the stages of producing a newspaper, using the present simple passive.

Someone ...
1 chooses a subject
2 writes an article
3 reads and checks the article
4 designs the pages
5 draws the pictures or takes the photos
6 scans the pictures or photos and puts them in the pages
7 sends the disc to the printer

1 *A subject is chosen.*
2 *An article is* ....
3 ....
4 ....
5 ....
6 ....
7 ....

2 Complete the magazine article with the present simple passive of the verbs in brackets.

YOUNG WRITERS

Sky reporter Jenny Roberts interviews one of the judges of the Young Writer of the Year Competition.

Q: How ¹*is the winner chosen* (the winner / choose)?

A: All the stories ² .... (read) by three judges and the twenty best stories ³ .... (choose). These ⁴ .... (send) to twelve students. The students ⁵ .... (ask) to give each story a mark out of ten. They ⁶ .... (not give) the name or age of the person who wrote them.

Q: How do you know that a mother or father didn't write the story?

A: You always know. A story which ⁷ .... (write) by a forty-year-old is different.

Q: ⁸ .... (the stories / print) in any magazine?

A: Yes, the prize-winning story ⁹ .... (always / print) in our magazine. The story ¹⁰ .... (usually / edit) first and the spelling ¹¹ .... (check) but the story ¹² .... (not / change) at all.

Q: Do people ever write picture stories?

A: Yes, one of the best stories this year is a cartoon. All the pictures ¹³ .... (draw) by a thirteen-year-old girl.

Q: What do the prize-winners get?

A: They ¹⁴ .... (not / give) money, they ¹⁵ .... (give) book tokens and they ¹⁶ .... (take) on a mystery trip round London.

Vocabulary revision

3 Complete the crossword.

Across
1. Let's play a ...... on the computer. (4)
3. You put this on the floor. (3)
5. What is this table made ...... ? (2)
7. Garden tables and chairs are often made of this. (7)
9. Can I have a ...... of tomato soup, please? (3)
11. I'd like a new ...... jacket. (7)
12. The ball won't break the window. It's made of .... (6)
14. Many houses in the north of Canada and the USA are made of .... (4)
16. Past tense of *hear*. (5)
18. Opposite of *yes*. (2)
19. I like wearing ...... in summer when it's very hot. (6)
20. A lot of kitchen ...... is recycled. (5)
22. Come in and ...... down. (3)
23. 09:20 = twenty ...... nine. (4)

Down
1. Would you like a ...... of lemonade? (5)
2. Gold is a type of .... (5)
4. Have you ...... the latest Blue CD? (3)
6. Synthetic ...... is a very strong material. (5)
7. It is best to take plastic or ...... plates and cups on a picnic. (5)
8. If you're going out, you'll need a warm .... (4)
10. I'm going to take a .... Smile and say *cheese*. (5)
13. Past tense of *burn*. (5)
14. A warm material. (4)
15. ...... and windows in a house are usually made of wood. (5)
16. ...... many bags of rubbish have we got? (3)
17. How much ...... the school magazine usually cost? (4)
21. I've just read ...... article about recycling. (2)

Villages were destroyed.

The past simple passive

1a Complete the magazine article with the correct verb in the past simple passive.

blow	fly	destroy
~~hit~~	injure	take
damage	kill	throw

TORNADO HITS KENTUCKY

On Sunday evening the state of Kentucky in the USA ¹ _was hit_ by a huge tornado. Winds in the town of Providence reached over 80 miles an hour. Thirty-two homes ² .... completely and a hundred and fourteen ³ .... Fortunately no one ⁴ .... but twelve people ⁵ ....

Most of these ⁶ .... to hospitals near Providence but one man ⁷ .... by helicopter to a hospital in Indiana. 'I've never seen such damage,' said 52-year-old George Schultz. 'The roof of the local public school ⁸ .... off and my car ⁹ .... ten metres into the air!'

1b Write questions and answers.

1 When / Kentucky / hit by a tornado?
2 How many homes / completely destroy?
3 How many homes / damage?
4 How many people / kill?
5 Where / most of the injured people / take?
6 How / one man / take / to a hospital?
7 What damage / do / to the school?
8 How / George's car / damage?

1 A: _When was Kentucky hit by a tornado?_
  B: _On Sunday evening._

2 A: ....
  ....
  B: ....

3 A: ....
  B: ....

4 A: ....
  B: ....

5 A: ....
  ....
  B: ....

6 A: ....
  ....
  B: ....

7 A: ....
  B: ....

8 A: ....
  B: ....

2a
Complete the sentences using the past simple passive of the verb in brackets. Then match the pictures to the correct sentences.

1 [B] The famous painting of the Mona Lisa _was damaged_ in 1956. (damage)
2 [ ] In 79AD, the Roman city of Pompeii .... by a volcanic explosion. (destroy)
3 [ ] The London Eye .... in 1999. (build)
4 [ ] Princess Diana .... in a car accident in 1997. (kill)
5 [ ] In 1969, the first moon landing .... on TV. (see)
6 [ ] In Ancient Greece, the Olympic flame .... into the Olympic stadium by a Greek athlete. (carry)

2b Write the questions for the answers.

1 Q: When _was the Mona Lisa damaged_ ?
   A: In 1956.
2 Q: How .... ?
   A: By a volcanic explosion.
3 Q: When .... ?
   A: In 1999.
4 Q: How .... ?
   A: In a car accident.
5 Q: What .... ?
   A: The first moon landing.
6 Q: What ....
   .... ?
   A: The Olympic flame.

Landscape

3a Circle the odd word out.
1 mountain (river) hill rock
2 lake sea ocean desert
3 cliff tree forest woods
4 beach coast valley sea
5 river stream tree ocean

3b Find fourteen words for landscape in this word puzzle.

M	O	U	N	T	A	I	N	F
I	C	L	I	F	F	O	C	O
S	E	A	O	C	R	W	S	R
L	A	K	E	O	O	O	T	E
A	N	H	L	A	C	O	R	S
N	B	I	D	S	K	D	E	T
D	I	L	G	T	H	S	A	K
V	A	L	L	E	Y	P	M	U
Y	D	E	S	E	R	T	O	N

He says we're leaving.

Reported statements in the present

1 Write sentences to report what the people are saying.

1 *He says he's going home now.*

2 She ....

3 ....

4 ....

5 ....

6 ....

7 ....

8 ....

Reported questions in the present

2a Write the direct questions.

Sam: 1 *Do you speak English?*
Barbara: Yes, I speak English.
Sam: 2 ....
Barbara: My name's Barbara.
Sam: 3 ....
Barbara: I come from Brazil.
Sam: 4 ....
Barbara: Yes, I'd like to see your school. Thank you.
Sam: 5 ....
Barbara: I'm staying here for three months.
Sam: 6 ....
Barbara: Yes, I can come to dinner tomorrow. Thank you.
Sam: 7 ....
Barbara: I like all sorts of food, but not fish and chips!

2b Rearrange the words to report Sam's questions.

1 English. speaks she if
  He wants to know *if she speaks English.*

2 is. name her what
  He wants to know ....

3 from. comes where she
  He wants to know ....

4 to like if school. she his would see
  He wants to know ....

5 staying how in she London. is long
  He wants to know ....

6 she tomorrow. come if can dinner to
  He wants to know ....

7 food sort she what likes. of
  He wants to know ....

Saying goodbye

3 Match the goodbye phrases in columns A and B.

A	B
1 Have a good holiday.	a Me too.
2 See you tomorrow.	b No, I won't.
3 I'm going to miss you.	c Yes, see you.
4 Remember to keep in touch.	d Thanks. I will.
5 Don't forget to send a postcard.	e Yes, I will.

| 1 | d | 2 | | 3 | | 4 | | 5 | |

Reported statements and reported questions

4 Sam and Lucy invite Ricky and Gina to go on a trip to Brighton. Read Gina's reply to Lucy and Sam and complete Lucy's note to her mother.

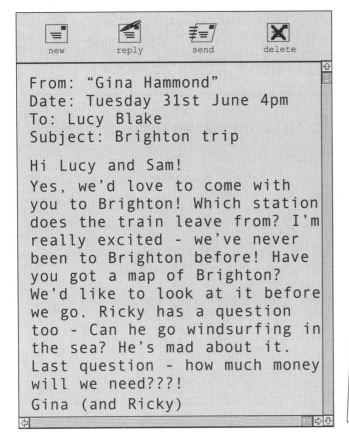

Mum

I've just had an email from Gina. She says that she and Ricky
¹ *would love to come* to Brighton with us and wants to know which station ² .... She's really excited. She says they
³ .... She wants to know ⁴ ....
.... a map of Brighton. She says ⁵ .... before they go. Then Ricky wants to know if ⁶ .... in the sea. Gina says ⁷ .... They also want to know ⁸ .... Can we talk about it when you get home at five o'clock?

Love
Lucy

Skills practice

New words
bamboo extinct gorilla
orang-utan poacher
turtle

Reading

ANIMALS IN DANGER

ORANG-UTANS
Orang-utans live in the tropical rain forests of Sumatra and Borneo. They are in danger because of poachers. Their babies are caught and are kept as pets or for scientific experiments. Their habitat is also in danger because trees are cut down and forests are burnt. The WWF (World Wide Fund for Nature) is studying orang-utans to see how we can help them live safely in the wild.

TURTLES
Turtles are sea animals which could become extinct. They live a long time. However, they are often caught in fishing nets and they die, or they are caught and eaten. Their eggs are stolen from their nests, and their nests are also destroyed. Sometimes rubbish is thrown in the sea. This can kill animals. For example, if a turtle eats a plastic bag, it will die. There are now campaigns to save the turtles and parts of some beaches are wildlife reserves for them.

PANDAS
Pandas live in bamboo forests in China. They used to live all over China, but they are now found only in the west of the country. Pandas can eat meat or plants, but they usually eat only bamboo. They eat thirty kilograms of bamboo in a day and often spend fourteen hours of each day eating. They are endangered because their habitat is destroyed and they do not have enough bamboo to eat. Sometimes they are hunted for their skins.

1a Read about the animals and answer True (✓) or False (✗).

1 Orang-utans are not in danger. ✗
2 Turtles don't live very long. ☐
3 Turtles lay eggs. ☐
4 Pandas don't eat bamboo. ☐
5 Hunters kill pandas for their skins. ☐

1b Match the phrases and write sentences.

1 Baby orang-utans — a are burnt.
2 Forests — b are found in west China.
3 Turtles — c are stolen from their nests.
4 Their eggs — d are kept as pets.
5 Pandas — e are often caught in fishing nets.

1 [d] Baby orang-utans are kept as pets.
2 ☐ ....
3 ☐ ....
4 ☐ ....
5 ☐ ....

Study tip
How to listen
Can you remember how to listen?

2 Complete the sentences with a word from the box.

> Concentrate   detail.   information.   know.
> meaning.   ~~predict~~   questions   worry

Try to ¹ ...predict... the information you are going to hear.
Make ² .... in your mind.
³ .... on the words which carry
⁴ ....
Don't ⁵ .... about the words you don't ⁶ ....
Listen more than once if you can. Listen first for general ⁷ ....
Then listen again for ⁸ ....

Writing

3 Complete the text with words from the box.

> ~~cruelly~~   frightened.   happier.
> Luckily   rescued   reserve.

Raffi and Anthea are a lion and lioness who were ¹ ...cruelly... put in a cage above a restaurant in Tenerife. They were very ² .... ³ .... they were ⁴ .... by the Born Free Foundation a few years ago. Now they are much ⁵ .... They live in a wildlife ⁶ ....

4 Now write another text about Twiggy the gorilla in your notebook. Use the prompts.

Twiggy / six-year-old / gorilla. Born / in forest / Cameroon. Mother and father / killed for meat. Twiggy / taken to Nigeria. She / sold / as pet. Luckily / rescued / Born Free Foundation. Now / she / happier. Live / wildlife centre / in Cameroon.

Cartoon Time:
Clark and Lois – school reporters

5 Complete the conversation with the words in the box.

> up   idea   says   bet   later   ~~guys~~   was

Lois: Hi, ¹ ...guys... . What's ² .... ?
Girl: The old piano ³ .... damaged so the school has bought a new one.
Boy: The teacher ⁴ .... that this new one is very expensive.

Girl: Do you want to help?
Clark: You ⁵ .... ! A new piano – that's a great story for the newspaper.
Lois: Good ⁶ ....

Boy: It's time for lunch. Let's go.
Lois: Hang on!
Girl: See you ⁷ ....

Check Lessons 36–39

1 Sam is helping in his local charity shop. Complete the sentences with the passive forms of the verbs.

We ¹ *are given* (give) old clothes and things which people don't want. The newer things ² .... (sell). They ³ .... (keep) over there. Books ⁴ .... (put) on the table at the front. Electrical goods ⁵ .... (not / sell) in the shop but ⁶ .... (give) away free to people who need them. The money ⁷ .... (take) from the customer and the goods ⁸ .... (put) in bags. Everything which ⁹ .... (not / sell) in a month ¹⁰ .... (recycle).

Score ___ /9

2 Find nine words.

P	L	A	S	T	I	C	R
T	H	K	L	O	P	O	U
A	G	L	A	S	S	T	B
M	E	T	A	L	F	T	B
W	O	O	D	T	M	O	E
O	P	A	P	E	R	N	R
O	B	H	J	I	O	L	E
L	E	A	T	H	E	R	N

Score ___ /8

3 Match the halves to make sentences.

1 Television was invented
2 Legolas was played
3 *Lord of the Rings* was made
4 The Harry Potter books were written
5 Australia was discovered
6 The 2002 World Cup was won
7 Britain was invaded

a by the Romans.
b by JK Rowling.
c in 1788.
d in New Zealand.
e by Brazil.
f by Orlando Bloom.
g by John Logie Baird.

| 1 | *g* | 2 | | 3 | | 4 | |
| 5 | | 6 | | 7 | |

Score ___ /6

4 The editor of *Fun!* magazine is talking about the Young Inventors Competition. Complete the text with the present or past passive forms of the verbs.

The Young Inventors Competition

The Young Inventors Competition ¹ *was started* (start) three years ago. Every year all the entries for the competition ² .... (read) by our judges. The winner ³ .... (choose) out of all the entries. We had a lot of entries this year. The first prize ⁴ .... (give) to the Schoolwork Robot which ⁵ .... (design) by Macey, and the second prize to the Super Skateboard which ⁶ .... (invent) by Harvey.

Score ___ /5

1. Where are you going?
2. What are you doing?
3. Why are you going there?
4. Who are you meeting?
5. How will you travel?
6. When will you be home?

5 What do Sam's parents want to know? Write sentences.

1. *My parents want to know where I am going.*
2. They want to know what ....
3. ....
4. ....
5. ....
6. ....

Score ___ /5

6 What does Ricky's penfriend want to know? Complete the sentences.

Hi Ricky,
I hope you're well! I'm doing a survey at school about life in England. Can you answer a few questions for me? Have you got a skateboard? Do you wear school uniform? Have you got a pet? Do you play football? Can you swim? Do you speak French? Do you like McFly? Please answer as soon as you can!
Best wishes,
Hans

1. *Hans wants to know if I can answer* a few questions.
2. He wants to know if I .... a skateboard.
3. He wants to know .... school uniform.
4. ....
   .... pet.
5. ....
   .... football.
6. ....
   .... swim.
7. ....
   .... French.
8. ....
   .... McFly.

Score ___ /7

CHECK YOUR SCORE!

TOTAL ___ /40

☐ Brilliant! (30–40)
☐ Good! (20–29)
☐ OK (10–19)

81

Puzzle Story 1   Lessons 1–10

Sally and the busker

It was the hottest day of the year and Sally Garner was shopping in town. She was looking for a present for her brother. She looked in the bookshop but her brother didn't like books. She looked in the record shop but she didn't know what music her brother liked. She looked in the sports shop but her brother didn't like sports. Now it was three o'clock in the afternoon and Sally was tired. She bought a bottle of water. Then she remembered: her brother liked computer games. She went to the computer shop to buy him a game.

There were some people in the computer shop. A young woman was talking to a shop assistant. The woman was wearing a T-shirt, jeans and trainers.

'How much is this laptop?' the woman asked.

'It's £700,' the shop assistant said.

'That's very expensive,' the woman said. 'I can't use a computer but I want to learn.'

There was another young woman in the shop. She was wearing a top, black trousers and trainers too. She was talking to another shop assistant.

'Is this a good game?' the woman asked.

'Yes,' the shop assistant said. 'It's very good and it's only £20. Do you want to buy it?'

'No,' the woman said. 'I haven't got any money today.'

Sally looked at the games in the shop and bought one called 'Amoeba Attack'. It was £15. She felt happy and she decided to talk to her friend George Blakely.

George was sitting outside the bank playing his guitar. He was a busker and he was blind. He sat there every day and played his guitar. He couldn't see but he could play the guitar very well and Sally loved his music.

'Hi, Sally. How are you?' George said.

'How did you know it was me?' Sally said.

'I can hear your shoes. You're wearing your sandals today. Am I right?'

Sally laughed. 'Yes, George. You're always right.'

Sally and George talked for a few minutes. Then a man came out of the bank. It was Mr Parker, the new bank manager.

'Mr Blakely, you can't play your guitar here,' he said.

'But George always plays his guitar here,' said Sally.

'He has to stop,' Mr Parker said. Then he walked into the bank.

'I'm sorry, George,' Sally said.

'Don't worry,' George said. 'I can find another place to play my guitar.'

Sally went into the bank to talk to Mr Parker again. Suddenly she heard a loud noise behind her.

'Don't look at me. Lie on the floor, NOW! I've got a gun.'

It was a bank robber. It was a woman's voice but Sally didn't look at her. Everybody lay on the floor quickly. Sally lay next to Mr Parker. His face was white. The robber took a lot of money from the bank and then ran out. All that Sally could see was the robber's trainers.

After a minute Sally stood up and went outside.

'George, someone stole some money from the bank,' Sally said. 'What did you hear?'

'A woman ran out of the bank one minute ago,' George said. 'She was wearing trainers. She ran into the Internet café next door.'

Sally walked into the Internet café. The café was full of people but there were only two women in trainers. They were the customers from the computer shop.

'Excuse me,' Sally said. 'What are you doing here?'

'I'm sending an email,' the woman in jeans and trainers said.

'And what are you doing here?' Sally said.

'I'm sending an email,' the woman in black trousers and trainers said.

Sally walked out of the café. Mr Parker was standing outside the bank.

'I know who stole the money!' Sally said.

'Who was it?' Mr Parker asked.

'First, I've got a question for you. Can George play his guitar here?'

'Yes,' Mr Parker said.

'Every day?' Sally asked.

'Yes, yes. Of course,' Mr Parker said. 'Who stole the money?'

George and Sally smiled.

> **New words**
> - busker • another • blind • manager
> - bank robber • gun

1 Answer the questions in your notebook.

1 What can't the woman in jeans do?
2 What hasn't the woman in black trousers got?
3 What was the bank robber wearing?
4 Where did the bank robber go?
5 What did the woman in jeans say when Sally asked: 'What are you doing here?'

2 Now solve the puzzle

Who is the bank robber?

a the woman in jeans
b the woman in black trousers

Puzzle Story 2

Lessons 11–20

The gold ring

'Your seat is 12D, over there, on the left,' the flight attendant said.

'Thank you,' Marcus said, and he walked down the aeroplane to his seat. It was a grey, cloudy day and Marcus was happy because he was travelling to Italy with his parents. It was a winter holiday.

Marcus sat down next to a tall man who was wearing jeans and a patterned sweater. Marcus said hello and got his book out of his bag. His parents were sitting in another row.

'What are you reading?' the man said.

'It's a ghost story,' Marcus said. 'What are you reading?'

'It's a biography of Kelvin Dayman, the famous footballer,' the man said. 'Here, you can have a look.'

Marcus took the biography and read one of the pages.

Kelvin's first international football match was in 2002. It was a great game. His team won 3–2 and Kelvin scored two goals. On that day he was wearing his favourite gold ring. It's thin and shiny and it's got a small, square diamond in it. It's his lucky ring and he always wears it when he plays football. After the international match Kelvin played two games for his club but then a Spanish club bought him for fifteen million euros. The club was called Real

'It's not very interesting,' Marcus said.

'I know,' the man said. 'I don't like Kelvin Dayman. His team beat my team in a tournament last year. He's on this plane today. Look.'

Marcus looked into the first-class section of the plane. Kelvin Dayman was sitting there. He was reading a magazine and he was wearing a smart, white tracksuit top with baggy, striped shorts and lots of jewellery.

'He's wearing a lot of jewellery,' Marcus said.

'Yes,' the man said. 'Kelvin Dayman loves jewellery. I buy and sell jewellery but I don't wear much.'

Marcus looked at the man. He was wearing two gold rings.

'This ring is very important for me,' the man said. 'My father gave it to me when I was fifteen years old. And I bought the other ring in Spain.'

Marcus read his book and ate dinner. After dinner Marcus went to the toilet. Kelvin Dayman and the man who was sitting next to Marcus were waiting for the toilet too. When Marcus finally went into the toilet, he saw something on the floor. He picked it up. It was a gold ring. It was thin and shiny and it had a round diamond on it. Marcus put the ring in his pocket and went back to his seat. He called the flight attendant.

'I've found a ring in the toilet,' Marcus said. 'It's a gold ring.'

The flight attendant took the ring and walked to the back of the plane. She picked up the microphone.

'Ladies and gentlemen, have you lost a gold ring? Someone has found a gold ring in the toilet. I have the ring here. Thank you very much.'

Kelvin Dayman got up and walked to the back of the plane. The man who was sitting next to Marcus got up too and walked to the back of the plane. Marcus could hear them.

'Excuse me,' Kelvin said. 'I've lost a gold ring.'

'Is this it, Mr Dayman?' the flight attendant said.

'Yes, that's it,' Kelvin said.

'Hang on,' the man who was sitting next to Marcus said. 'That's my gold ring.'

'What's your name?' the flight attendant said.

'Patrick,' he said. 'And that's my ring. I bought it last year when I was in Spain.'

'But that's my ring,' Kelvin said. 'It's my favourite gold ring and I always wear it when I play football.'

Marcus stood up and walked to the back of the plane.

'Excuse me,' he said. 'I can help.'

> **New words**
> - flight attendant • row • ring
> - diamond • lucky • jewellery
> - microphone

1 Answer the questions in your notebook.

1 The man who is sitting next to Marcus is reading a book. What is the book?
2 Kelvin Dayman was wearing a ring when he played his first international football match. What was it like?
3 What does Marcus find in the toilet and what is it like?
4 Who does Marcus give the ring to?
5 Who says that the ring is his?

2 Now solve the puzzle.

Whose does the ring belong to?
a Kelvin Dayman   b The tall man

Puzzle Story 3

Lessons 21–30

Internet threat!

Lizzie Edwards was reading a book in her living room. Her mother, father and little sister, Katie, were watching a soap on TV.

'Soaps are boring,' her father said. 'Let's watch a western.'

'No,' Katie said. 'Westerns are boring. Let's watch MTV.'

'MTV is boring,' said Lizzie's mother. 'Let's watch a musical.'

Lizzie stopped reading her book. Her family had the same conversation every evening.

'If you stop watching TV and read a book, you'll be much happier,' said Lizzie. But her family weren't listening. Lizzie got up and went to her bedroom. She turned on her computer and went online. Lizzie used her computer to do her homework and to chat to her friends on an instant message service. Her screen name was 'WildChild'. An Internet friend was online too.

Instant chat — EXIT CHAT ROOM

Topic: Tennis

<FabFreddy> Hello, Wildchild. How are you?

<Wildchild> Hi, FabFreddy. I'm fine but my family are driving me crazy! And there's a tennis tournament on Friday. I really want to win it.

<FabFreddy> Don't worry. Give me your phone number and we can talk about it.

Lizzie laughed. She was clever and she never gave her personal details to anyone on the Internet.

Topic: Tennis

<Wildchild> No thanks, FabFreddy. If you are my friend, you won't ask for my personal details again.

Another person wanted to talk to Lizzie online. Her name was 'RudeGirl'.

Topic: Tennis

<RudeGirl> Hello, Wildchild. I know your name. You're Lizzie Edwards.

<Wildchild> Who are you? How do you know my name?

<RudeGirl> You think you're clever but you're not. I'm cleverer than you. Have you checked your emails today?

Lizzie checked her emails. There was only one email, from rudegirl@newmail.com.

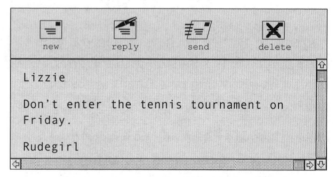

new   reply   send   delete

Lizzie

Don't enter the tennis tournament on Friday.

Rudegirl

Lizzie turned off her computer and picked up her book. But she couldn't forget about Rudegirl. Who was she? How did she know Lizzie's IMS screen name? Only Lizzie's friends, family and classmates knew that. She showed the email to her family but they didn't want to read it. They were watching TV.

The next day Lizzie went to school. At lunchtime she sat with her friends and told them about Rudegirl. In the afternoon they had English. Lizzie liked her English teacher.

'What would you like to be?' the teacher asked.

'I'd like to be a TV reporter,' one girl said.

'I'd like to be a ski instructor,' another girl said.

'I'd like to be a detective,' Lizzie said.

That evening Lizzie checked her emails again. There was another email from Rudegirl.

```
Lizzie

Don't forget, don't enter the tennis
tournament on Friday. Read detective
stories if you want to be a detective
but don't play tennis.

Rudegirl
```

Lizzie thought about the email for a minute. Rudegirl knew that Lizzie wanted to be a detective. That meant that Rudegirl was one of Lizzie's classmates. Only two girls in Lizzie's class played tennis: Claire and Tara. Lizzie had an idea.

The next day in school, Lizzie went into her classroom and sat next to Claire.

'Are you entering the tennis tournament on Friday?' Lizzie asked.

'Yes, I am,' Claire said.

'Me too,' Lizzie said. 'I've got new trainers. Good luck in the tournament!'

In the afternoon Lizzie sat next to Tara.

'Are you entering the tennis tournament on Friday?' Lizzie asked.

'Yes, I am,' Tara said. 'Are you?'

'Yes, I am,' Lizzie said. 'I've got a new tennis racket. The tournament will be fun.'

That evening Lizzie went home. She turned on her instant message service. Rudegirl was online.

```
Topic: Tennis

<Rudegirl> Don't enter the tennis
tournament on Friday, Lizzie. I'm going
to win it.

<Wildchild> I'm good at tennis. I may
win it!

<Rudegirl> You won't win it. You've
got a new racket but I'm better at
tennis. I'll win.

<Wildchild> I doubt it! See you
tomorrow.
```

Lizzie smiled and picked up her book. 'I'll be a good detective,' she thought.

New words
- personal details
- (enter a) tournament
- classmates
- instant message service (IMS)

1 Answer the questions in your notebook.

1 What is Lizzie doing on Friday?
2 What does Rudegirl say to Lizzie in her email?
3 What did Lizzie tell Claire?
4 What did Lizzie tell Tara?

2 Now solve the puzzle.

Who is Rudegirl?
a Claire **b** Tara
How do you know?

Puzzle Story 4 — Lessons 31–40

The chemical company and the beach

'Come on Carl,' Adam said. 'It's the weekend and we're going to surf all day!'

'You bet!' Carl said, and he picked up his surfboard and ran after Adam.

Carl and Adam were mad about surfing. During the week they went to school but every weekend they went surfing. Adam was captain of the school football team and Carl was a journalist for the school newspaper, *The Longbeach Gazette*.

'If I didn't go to school, I'd go surfing every day,' Adam said.

'Me too,' Carl said, 'but I'd write articles for the newspaper too. Hey, who are they? They're in a bad mood.'

Two other boys were surfing in the sea. One of the boys was shouting at Adam and Carl. He was angry.

'That's Victor Sanders and Simon Vallence,' said Adam. 'They think that this is their beach.'

'What are you doing here?' Victor said. 'We're surfing here.'

Adam and Carl laughed. 'This is everyone's beach,' said Adam, 'and everyone can surf here. If you don't like it, go home.'

Adam and Carl ran into the sea and started surfing. They surfed for about two hours but then Carl stopped surfing and lay down on the sand.

'What's the matter?' Adam asked.

'I've got a headache and a sore throat,' Carl said.

'Me too,' Adam said. 'I think we should stop surfing, just to be sure.'

Then Adam saw two barrels on the sand. The boys went to look at them. They were made of metal and were full of chemicals. Some of the chemicals were spilling into the sea.

'This is why we're ill,' Adam said. 'The sea is polluted with chemicals. But where are these barrels from?'

'I don't know,' said Carl, 'but I'm going to find out and then I'm going to write an article for the newspaper about it.'

The boys walked home. Adam called his friends and told them not to go surfing. Carl went online and started surfing the Internet. After

ten minutes he found a website about chemical companies in Longbeach. There were two chemical companies: Standard Chemicals and Rotex Chemicals.

'But which chemical company is polluting the beach?' asked Adam.

'I don't know,' said Carl, 'but I've got an idea.'

That evening, about ten o'clock, Adam and Carl went to the beach again. They were carrying a torch and some food and they were wearing warm clothes. They sat down near the car park and waited. About two o'clock in the morning they heard a lorry. The lorry came into the car park and two men got out.

'This is a public beach,' the first man said. 'Why are we leaving the barrels here?'

'Because Mr Sanders says that we have to,' the second man said. 'Now stop asking questions and help me with these barrels.'

The two men began to take metal barrels off the lorry and put them on the beach. Carl and Adam stood up.

'Hey, what are you doing?' Adam said.

The two men got into the lorry quickly and drove away.

'Stop!' Carl said, but the men didn't stop.

The next day Carl and Adam went to the beach again. They didn't go surfing, they just sat on the beach and talked.

'We still don't know which company those barrels are from,' Carl said.

'I know,' Adam said, 'but we're going to find out.'

Then the two boys saw Victor and his friend again. They were wearing their wetsuits and carrying their surfboards.

'Don't go in the sea,' Adam said. 'It's polluted. There are chemicals in the sea.'

'Don't be silly,' Victor said. 'My dad is manager of Standard Chemicals and Simon's uncle is manager of Rotex Chemicals. There aren't any chemicals in this sea.' Victor and Simon ran into the sea and started surfing.

'That's interesting,' Carl said. 'I think I can write my article now.'

New words
- wetsuit • barrel • torch
- public beach

1 Answer the questions in your notebook.

1 What did Carl and Adam find on the beach?
2 What are the names of the two boys who Adam and Carl talked to?
3 Why was the lorry in the car park?
4 What did the second man in the lorry say?
5 Who is Victor's dad and who is Simon's uncle?

2 Now solve the puzzle.

Which company put the barrels of chemicals on the beach?

a Standard Chemicals   b Rotex Chemicals

The science-fiction comedy horror western musical

A play to act after Lesson 20

Characters
Director   Sally   Soundman
Cameraman Barman   Sheriff
Alien 1   Alien 2 Cowboys
Cowgirls

New words
- cowboy • cowgirl • film scene
- saloon • parking ticket • Sheriff
- script

The scene is a film set. It's a saloon in a western. Filming hasn't started yet. All the actors and actresses are talking to each other.

Director: OK, everybody, thank you for coming. Today we are going to start making my new film. It's called *The Cowgirl and the Alien*. It's a science-fiction comedy horror western musical.

Cowboy 1: Did you say a 'science-fiction comedy horror western musical'?

Director: That's right. A science-fiction comedy horror western musical. Now, have you all learnt your lines?

All: Yes.

Director: OK, good. Go to your places, please.

The actors and actresses go to their places. There are three tables with cowboys and cowgirls at each table. There is a long bar and a barman.

Director: OK, is everyone ready?

All: Yes.

Director: Great! Here goes: lights, camera, action!

Sally is off stage. The barman is cleaning the bar. The cowboys and cowgirls are playing cards. They start to sing this song to the tune of 'Don't worry, be happy' and each table stands up when they sing their lines.

Table 1: Here's a little song we wrote,
You might want to sing it, note for note,

Table 2: Be careful, of Sally.

Table 3: She's the girl who likes no one,
She wears a hat and she carries a gun.

Table 2: Be careful of Sally.

Cowboy 1: Ohhhh, ohh, ohh, ohh, ohhh ...

Director: Cut, cut, cut. Must you?

Cowboy 1: What?

Director: Sing?

Cowboy 1: Sorry. I was hopeless. I'm not going to sing any more.

Director: Good. OK, from the beginning: lights, camera, action!

The cowboys and cowgirls start the scene again from the beginning. At the end of the song Sally walks in and everyone stops talking and looks at her. She looks very angry and mean.

Sally: Are you the person who put a parking ticket on my horse?

Cowgirl 1: No, Sally. It wasn't me.

Sally: Who was it? WHO WAS IT? ... Never mind. It's too quiet in here. Talk!

Everyone starts talking, playing cards again and making a lot of noise. Sally walks over to the bar.

Sally: It's TOO LOUD in here. Keep quiet. Barman, give me a glass of milk.

Barman: Here you are and here's your change.

Table 1: She used to be a sweet young child,
But now she's mean and very wild,

Table 2: Be careful, of Sally.

Table 3: She doesn't call anyone 'Sir',
Even the Sheriff is scared of her.

Table 2: Be careful, of Sally.

Cowboy 1: Ohhhh, ohh, ohh, ohh, ohhh ...

Director: Cut, cut!

Cowboy 1: Oh, I'm very sorry. I forgot. I'm going to keep quiet.

Director: Thank you. OK, everyone, from the beginning. Lights, camera, action!

Everyone starts the scene again from the beginning. At the end of the second song the Sheriff runs in. He is very scared.

Cowgirl 2: Look, there's the Sheriff.

Sheriff: Quick, run!

Cowboy 2: What's happening, Sheriff?

Sheriff: An alien has landed. He's silver and he's got a round shiny head. I couldn't stop him. He's going to eat us!

Sally: Don't exaggerate, Sheriff.

Alien 1 walks in carrying a book.

Director: Cut, cut! Why are you carrying a book?

Alien 1: Oh, sorry. I forgot. I was waiting outside and I was a bit bored so I was reading this book. It's a great book. It's a romantic novel. It's about ...

Director: I'm trying to make a film and you aren't helping. Aliens DON'T READ! OK, everyone. From the beginning. Lights, camera, action!

Everyone does the scene again from the beginning. This time a different alien walks in. It's a real alien but nobody knows this. The cowboys and cowgirls start shooting at the alien but nothing stops him. When the alien points at them, they fall on the floor. Finally, only Sally is still standing. The alien walks over to Sally.

Sally: OK, alien. It's just you and me now.

Alien 2: Grrrrrr. Hrrrrr.

Sally: I'm not scared of you.

Alien 2: Rarrrrrrrrr.

Sally: You've got very big eyes. I like your eyes. Do you like my eyes?

Alien 2: Hmmmmmm.

Director: Hang on! This isn't in the script.

Sally: Wow! I think I love you. Do you love me?

Alien 2: Hmmmmmmmmmm.

Director: Have you gone mad? This isn't in the script! Cut, cut!

Sally: I've waited all my life to meet someone like you.

Alien 2: Grrrrrrrrrrrrr.

Sally: Come on! Let's go and have a coffee.

Director: Cut, cut! What are you doing?

Sally and the alien hold hands and start to walk off the stage. The director tries to stop them but the alien points at him and he falls on the floor. The alien points at the cameraman and soundman and they fall on the floor too. Sally and the alien walk off the stage. After a short time, Alien 1 walks on carrying his book again.

Alien 1: I'm really sorry. I started reading my book and I forgot about the film and ... What's happened here?

The watch that stops time

A play to act after Lesson 40

Characters
Erin
Jack
Mr Tunity
Stallholders
Mrs Regis
Students

New words
- stall • special • strap • press
- cheat • crawl • opportunity
- zero

Erin and Jack are on the way to school. They are walking through a market. They walk past a man who is selling old things on a stall. Jack stops.

Erin: Hurry up, Jack. We're late for the Geography exam. If we fail this exam, we'll …

Jack: I know, I know, we'll have to take the exam again in our summer holidays.

Erin: Have you studied for the exam?

Jack: No, I haven't. Have you?

Erin: Not much. I'm a bit worried about this exam. I'm not keen on Geography but I don't want to take the exam again in my summer holiday.

Jack: Hey, Erin, look at this stall.

Mr Tunity: Good afternoon, my name is Mr Tunity. How can I help you?

Jack: Well, I really need a watch.

Erin: That's true, he does. He's always late.

Mr Tunity: Well, I have a beautiful watch, but I can only sell this watch to a special person. Someone who is sensible.

Erin: We're sensible!

Mr Tunity: And someone who is very, very honest?

Jack: Yes, we're very honest. Can we see the watch?

Mr Tunity: Well, OK. But first you have to pay me for the watch. It's £10.

Jack: I've got £5. Have you got £5, Erin?

Erin: Yes, here you are.

Mr Tunity: Thank you. And here is the watch.

 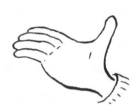

Erin: But that's just a boring old watch. It's made of glass and metal and the strap is made of leather. It's not special!

Mr Tunity: It's very special. If you press this button, time stops.

Jack: Don't be silly. Nothing can stop time.

Mr Tunity: This watch can.

Erin: Come on Jack, we're late.

Mr Tunity: Remember, you can only press the button once.

Jack: OK, Mr Tunity.

Mr Tunity: And you must be sensible and honest, very, very honest.

Erin: Thanks, Mr Tunity.

Mr Tunity: Please, call me Opor. I'll see you again soon.

Jack: Bye, Opor.

Erin: Bye, Opor.

In a classroom at school. Jack and Erin are taking an exam. Jack is at the back of the classroom and Erin is at the front. There are a lot of other students and there is a teacher at the front of the class.

Mrs Regis: OK, class. Today is your Geography exam. If you fail this exam, you have to take it again in your summer holidays. Do you understand?

Class: Yes, Mrs Regis.

Mrs Regis: Don't talk or cheat in this exam. If you talk or cheat, you'll fail the exam. Do you understand?

Class: Yes, Mrs Regis.

Mrs Regis: Good! Start now.

Mrs Regis reads a book in her chair at the front of the class. Jack holds his head in his hands. He can't answer any of the questions. He waves to Erin but she can't see him. Jack crawls over to Erin.

Jack: What's the answer to Question 1?

Mrs Regis: Jack! Erin! You're cheating! That's very bad. I'm going to …

Jack: Stop!

Jack presses the button on his watch and everyone stops. They are all like statues. Only Jack and Erin can move and talk.

Erin: What's happened? Why has everybody stopped?

Jack: I pressed the button on this watch and time stopped.

Erin: What shall we do?

Jack: Let's look at the answers. Here they are, on Mrs Regis's desk.

Erin: But that's cheating.

Jack: Yes, but no one will see us.

Erin: OK.

Jack and Erin copy the answers from Mrs Regis's desk. There's a knock on the door. Erin opens the door. Mr Tunity is standing there. He doesn't look pleased.

Jack: Opor! What are you doing here?

Erin: Jack pressed the button on the watch.

Mr Tunity: I can see. So, what did you do when you pressed the button? Did you help other people or did you help yourselves?

Jack, Erin: Err …

Mr Tunity: Were you honest or did you try to cheat in the exam?

Erin: Err … we tried to cheat.

Mr Tunity: What's my name?

Erin: It's Opor. Opor Tunity. Gosh! Opportunity.

Mr Tunity: You had an opportunity but you were greedy. Now, for the first time today, I want you to do the right thing. Then you can bring me the watch this evening.

Jack: OK, Opor.

Mr Tunity leaves.

Erin: What are we going to do?

Jack: We're going to tell Mrs Regis that we cheated and we're going to do the exam again in our summer holiday.

Erin: Yes, but this time we're going to study hard and we're going to pass.

Jack: Good plan!

Jack and Erin go back to Erin's desk. Jack presses the button on the watch again. All the students start writing again and Mrs Regis continues.

Jack: Start!

Mrs Regis: … give you zero for this exam and you're going to …

Erin: We're going to take this exam again in our summer holidays.

Mrs Regis: Yes, that's right.

Jack: That's OK, Mrs Regis. We're going to pass it next time!

Songs

 **I'm a music fan
(Lessons 1–5)**

Sometimes I play basketball,
Rugby, tennis or football,
Sometimes I just ride my bike to school.
But there's one thing I always do,
When playing sport or being cool,
I listen to my Discman,
I'm a music fan.

I listen to rock, I listen to rap, I listen to
   pop,
In the park, in the café, and in the shop,
When I go swimming, when I go karting,
   and on the beach.
Yes I am, yes I am, I'm a music fan.

I went out last Saturday,
I went to see a new band play,
I thought they were so cool that I brought
   them home.
Now they're living in my room,
Mum says they must leave real soon,
But I don't think they can,
'Cos I'm a music fan.

 **My coat with the strange design
(Lessons 11–15)**

I bought a coat which has a
   very strange design,
I bought it from a man who
   said it looked just fine.
I bought it in a shop where
   clothes are very cheap,
I bought it for just 50p.

It was checked on the front
   and spotted on the back.
It was blue and green and
   red and pink and black.
It was long and loose and
   not so very smart,
But I loved it with all my heart.

I saw a science-fiction film at the cinema,
There were aliens who came from very far,
They could fly and walk on water like a boat,
But the strangest thing there was my new coat.

 **The best day so far
(Lessons 16–20)**

I've flown round the whole world on an aeroplane,
I've travelled to China on a railway train,
I've driven a Porsche and a Ferrari car,
But today is the best (best) day that I've had so far.

I've seen the wonders of this big wide world,
I've met handsome men and I've met pretty girls,
I've watched the night sky with its moon and stars,
But today is the best (best) day that I've had so far.

There are some things that take your breath away,
For all of these things you never have to pay,
But it doesn't matter, my friend, where you are,
Because today is the best (best) day you've had so
   far.

**Technology will do it all
(Lessons 21–25)**

In the future when we are at home,
We will download movies on our mobile phone,
We will clean the house,
With one click of the mouse,
Technology will do it all.

Looking back on times that have passed,
There were no PCs and life wasn't so fast,
But now the world has changed, things don't stay the same,
Do you think that it's a shame?

Years from now when we all work from home,
We won't meet face to face, we'll just talk on the phone,
Plumbers won't fix drains,
Pilots won't fly planes,
Technology will do it all.

Looking back on times that have passed,
There were no PCs and life wasn't so fast,
But now the world has changed, things don't stay the same,
Do you think that it's a shame?

 **Let's go online
(Lessons 31–35)**

If you had a big sailing yacht,
Would you invite me to an island that's hot?
And if you were a multimillionaire,
Would you still enjoy the times that we share?

We are fond of each other,
Good at working together,
Loyal, like sister and brother,
Because we're mad about the same thing, so

Let's go online,
And meet in cyberspace,
Let's go online,
I've never seen your face,
Let's go online,
Because when you're there for me online,
I know that everything is fine.

If I you had a smart, pretty wife,
Would you still have time for online chat in your life?
And if you had a nice black motorbike,
Would you invite me to all the places you like?

**My little island is
starting to sink
(Lessons 36–40)**

I found a little island,
Out in the middle of the sea.
Twenty people lived there,
Twenty-one with me.

The people there were happy,
With a smile on each face,
But then someone opened,
A little fast-food place.

The fast-food place makes a lot
   of cash,
But we can't move because of all
   the trash,
The plastic containers, the cans for
   the drinks,
My little island is starting to sink.

It used to be so pretty,
Our island in the sea.
There was no pollution,
And all the food was free.

Coconuts were picked,
from the coconut tree.
Tasty fish were caught,
from the lake near me.

The fast-food place makes a lot
   of cash,
But we can't move because of all
   the trash,
The plastic containers, the cans for
   the drinks,
My little island is starting to sink.

I found a little island,
Out in the middle of the sea.
Twenty people lived there,
But now not me!

Pearson Education Limited,
Edinburgh Gate, Harlow
Essex, CM20 2JE, England
and Associated Companies throughout the world

www.longman.com

© Pearson Education Limited, 2005

All rights reserved: no part of this publication may be reproduced, stored in a retrieval system, or transmitted in any form or by any means, electronic, mechanical, photocopying, recording or otherwise without the prior permission of the copyright holders.

The rights of Ingrid Freebairn, Hilary Rees-Parnall and Jonathan Bygrave to be identified as the authors of this work have been asserted by them in accordance with the Copyright, Designs and Patents Act 1988.

First published 2005
Second impression 2005
Set in 12.5pt Bliss Light
Printed in Spain
By Mateu Cromo, S.A. Pinto (Madrid)
Prepared for publication by Stenton Associates

Designed by Michael Harris

ISBN 0 582 838665
      0 582 838975 (with CD)

Acknowledgements

Illustrators:

Tim Archbold (Graham-Cameron Illustration); Kathy Baxendale; Humberto Blanco (Sylvie Poggio); Neil Chapman (Beehive Illustration); Peter Dennis (Linda Rogers Associates); Phil Garner (Beehive Illustration); Brett Hudson (Graham-Cameron Illustration); Joanna Kerr; Andy Keylock (Beehive Illustration); Martin Sanders (Beehive Illustration); Theresa Tibbetts (Beehive Illustration); Tony Wilkins.

We are grateful to the following for permission to reproduce photographs:

©De Agostini/NHMPL page 18 left; Alamy/Photofusion/PaulBaldesare page 3; Alamy/Suzy Bennet page 38 top; Alamy/Photofusion Picture Library page 48 left; Alamy/Carlos Villoch page 78 centre; ©Atlanta Constitution/CORBIS SYGMA page 74; ©British Board of Film Classification page 69; ©CORBIS SYGMA page 78 right; Digital Vision page 48 right; Empics/Adam Davy page 67; Getty Images/Hulton Archive page17; Nick Hewetson©Dorling Kindersley page 19; ©Jack Hollingsworth/CORBIS page 68 right; Angelo Hornak/CORBIS PAGE 35; ©Milepost 92 1/2 page 38 bottom; ©The Natural History Museum, London page 18 right; ©Stan Osolinksi/CORBIS page 78 left; Rex Features/Peter Brooker page 11; Stone/Ken Fisher page 48 centre; Taxi/Bavaria page 68 centre; Taxi/Bill Losh page 68 left.

Every effort has been made to trace the copyright holders and we apologise in advance for any unintentional omissions. We would be pleased to insert the appropriate acknowledgement in any subsequent edition of this publication.